Sacred Ceremony

Create and Officiate
Personalized Wedding Ceremonies

dayna reid

Dedication

I am so very grateful and appreciative of my daughter Shayla and my son Delane. While they are vastly different in their outlooks and roads chosen in life, each one's unique strength of character, values, and love have consistently supported and encouraged me on my own life path. They continuously remind me of what is possible when you are deeply loved.

Contents

Introduction

Did you know that you can fully customize not only the vows, but *all* the words spoken during your ceremony? When planning a wedding, there are many resources available to assist you with all the details to make it a *visual* dream, but what about the ceremony itself? Wouldn't you like the same attention to detail and extensive variety of personalized choices for the most important aspect of your wedding—the *words* spoken to seal your commitment to each other?

Within these pages you will find everything you need to easily create and conduct a ceremony that genuinely expresses to your guests what your beliefs are about the significance of marriage and accurately communicates the true intentions of the promises you wish to make to each other.

Who should read this book?

This book provides you (the couple getting married or renewing their vows) as well as officiants or ministers with all the information needed to compose and carry out a truly meaningful wedding ceremony, including information on selecting an Officiant (or becoming ordained if you wish to have a friend or family member officiate the ceremony or wish to officiate weddings as a business), obtaining the marriage license and filing the paperwork.

How to use this book

You may choose to start with learning all about "Making It Legal," or you may choose to go directly to the "Wedding Ceremony Elements Overview" section which describes the traditional wedding ceremony elements and the meaning behind each one, aiding you in deciding what to include and what to leave out of your ceremony.

Once you have selected the elements that are important to you, each one has its own section in the book with both spiritual and non-spiritual wording options. To compliment the traditional elements, there are many alternatives for including additional touches, such as a Candle Lighting Ceremony, Rose Ceremony, remembering loved ones unable to attend or including children.

A worksheet is included at the end of the book to assist with compiling your ceremony wording choices as you progress through the book. Sample ceremonies (including vow renewal ceremonies) are also provided. You may choose one of the samples for your wedding, or simply as a starting point to generate ideas for composing your ceremony. Note: All wording can be easily altered for use in a Renewal of Vows ceremony.

Now let's begin the journey of designing the ceremony that expresses your deepest desire for each other and your marriage …

5 Steps to Creating Your Personalized Ceremony

Follow these five steps to create your own unique and personalized wedding ceremony:

1. Read through the "Wedding Ceremony Elements Overview" section and select the elements you wish to include in your ceremony.

2. Read through the "Ceremony Elements Selections" section for each element that you selected in Step 1 based on your spiritual or non-spiritual wording preference. Record your choices on the Worksheet at the end of this book.

3. Read through the "Additional Ceremony Elements" section and decide if you wish to include any of these symbolic ceremonies. Record your choices on the Worksheet.

4. Read through the "Reading Selections" section and select the Readings you wish to include. Record your choices on the Worksheet.

5. Complete the remaining "Music Selection" sections on the Worksheet with the choices you have made about the music to include in your ceremony. These decisions are usually coordinated with the business service providing the music (i.e. Disc Jockey, Harpist, Pianist, Vocalist, etc.).

Once you have completed these steps, follow the "Considerations When Selecting an Officiant" section of this book for choosing someone to conduct your ceremony.

Wedding Ceremony Elements Overview

There are many elements to choose from when creating your ceremony, but there are only two elements that are legally required: the Declaration of Intent and the Pronouncement of marriage. In other words, you could literally have a ceremony that read: "Jane, do you agree to marry Joe? And Joe, do you agree to marry Jane? I now pronounce you married." All other elements are optional, which gives you tremendous flexibility in designing a ceremony that is the most meaningful to the two of you.

In addition to the basic elements of a traditional ceremony, there are many other special touches that can be added to your ceremony to make it unique and your own, such as including children, honoring parents or grandparents, remembering loved ones that are unable to attend or have passed on, etc. (see the "Additional Ceremony Elements" and "Ideas for Personalizing Your Wedding Ceremony" sections of this book for more ideas on customizing your Wedding).

Traditional Ceremony Elements and Their Purposes

As you read through the description for each of the traditional ceremony elements in this section, you may choose which elements to include and which ones to leave out of your ceremony.

Procession

(also known as the Wedding March)

This is the choreographed walk down the aisle of the wedding party to the altar. This symbolically represents two things: the couple's transition from their individual lives to the union of marriage and the wedding attendants' support of the union by taking part in the same walk.

The Officiant, Groom and Best Man wait at the altar for the wedding party to walk down the aisle in the following order: first the Groomsmen paired with the Bridesmaids, followed by the Maid or Matron of Honor, then the Ring Bearer, then the Flower Girl, and lastly the Bride and her Father. Facing the altar, the women will be on the left and the men will be on the right.

In addition, traditionally, the guests will be seated on the same side of the altar as the one (bride or groom) who invited them. Music played for the Procession can be a single selection or multiple selections (a selection for the wedding party and a different selection for the Bride, etc.).

Order of Procession

(Keep in mind that it is your wedding and you may arrange your wedding party in any order you choose.)

Officiant/Minister ▢ ◯ **Groom**

◯ Best Man

Bridesmaid ◯ ◯ Groomsman

Bridesmaid ◯ ◯ Groomsman

Bridesmaid ◯ ◯ Groomsman

◯ Maid/Matron of Honor

◯ Ring Bearer

◯ Flower Girl

Bride ◯ ◯ Bride's Father

Order at the Altar

(Keep in mind that it is your wedding and you may arrange your wedding party in any order you choose.)

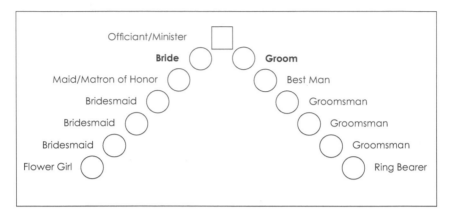

Approval Blessing

(also known as the "Give Away")

This element gives others the opportunity to give their approval or blessing on the ceremony that is about to take place. Traditionally the father or the parents of the Bride answer "I do" or "We do" to a question asked by the Officiant.

Welcome/Introduction

(also known as the Convocation)

This element calls together all in attendance to begin the ceremony. The words spoken at this time welcome and thank the guests as well as introduce the purpose of this gathering.

Opening Blessing

(a prayer also known as the Invocation)

The words spoken at this time are intended to invoke a higher source (God, Goddess, Great Spirit, the Universe, etc.) to elevate the intent of the ceremony.

The Address

(also known as the Sermon)

This element shares with the guests, the couple's beliefs on the meaning of marriage, and is designed to encourage reflection on the significance of this commitment. This may also include a historical reflection on the couple's relationship up until this point, as well as the story of how the couple met.

Dedication Blessing

(a prayer also known as the Consecration)

The words spoken at this time are meant to elevate the intent of the message communicated in the Address and remind everyone that the commitment about to be made is sacred.

This element also provides a transition from the message about marriage just spoken to the actual promises that the couple is about to make to seal their commitment.

Declaration of Intent

(a legally required element of the ceremony)

This element is the "I Do" section of the ceremony. The words spoken at this time declare the couple's intention to marry. The declaration is customarily made by the Bride and Groom, each answering "I do" or "I will" in response to a question presented by the Officiant.

The Vows

This element is the verbal exchange between the couple that expresses the sincere promises they are making to each other regarding their intention for the marriage.

The words spoken at this time may be memorized, read from paper, or recited after the Officiant.

Ring Blessing

The words spoken at this time describe the purpose of exchanging the rings and the sentiment that the couple wishes to be reminded of as they wear them.

Exchanging of the Rings

This element is the physical exchange of wedding rings and the verbal exchange between the couple that expresses the significance of this offering. The words spoken at this time may be memorized, read from paper, or recited after the Officiant.

Pronouncement of Marriage

(a legally required element of the ceremony)

This element is the pronouncement that the couple is officially wed.

The Kiss

This element is a kiss shared between the couple and symbolically represents the sealing of the promises made. The words spoken at this time instruct the couple to kiss.

Closing Blessing

(a prayer also known as the Benediction)

The words spoken at this time are meant to send the couple off into their new future together, and to communicate the hopes and wishes for that future.

The Presentation

This element is the official introduction of the newly married couple.

The Recession

This element is the choreographed walk down the aisle of the wedding party away from the altar and to the festivities. This walk signifies the completion of the ceremony and the beginning of the celebration. Traditionally, the wedding party exits in the opposite order they entered with the Bride and Groom exiting first.

Order of Recession

(Keep in mind that it is your wedding and you may arrange your wedding party in any order you choose.)

Officiant/Minister ☐

Bridesmaid ◯ ◯ Groomsman

Bridesmaid ◯ ◯ Groomsman

Bridesmaid ◯ ◯ Groomsman

Best Man ◯ ◯ Maid/Matron of Honor

◯ Ring Bearer

◯ Flower Girl

Bride ◯ ◯ **Groom**

Readings and Additional Ceremony Elements

Readings consist of one or more selections (poems, lyrics, stories, etc.) to be read aloud during carefully selected moments throughout the ceremony. The selections are meant to convey a feeling or message that provides a window into the couple's unique world and may be read by a friend, family member or the Officiant. Readings may also be incorporated into the ceremony as the wording for one of the traditional ceremony elements.

Additional Ceremony Elements are special purpose mini ceremonies that are performed to further symbolically demonstrate any commitments or statements you wish to communicate. For example, a Candle Lighting Ceremony (the lighting of a single unity candle, by the bride and groom with individual taper candles) may be included to symbolize the joining together of two lives into one.

Ceremony Element Selections

Approval Blessings

Who presents _____ to be married to _____?

❖

Who presents this woman to be wed?

❖

Who brings this woman to marry this man?

❖

Who gives this woman in marriage?

❖

Who gives their blessing for this marriage?

❖

Who gives their support for this marriage?

❖

Who gives their blessing on this union between _____ and ____?

❖

Who gives their support for this union between _____ and ____?

❖

Welcome/Introductions

Spiritual Introductions

_____ and _____ want to welcome you to this celebration of their love for one another. Each of you has given something special to their lives. Your love and encouragement will forever be appreciated. Thank you for sharing one of life's most sacred moments with them. May you be as important a part of their tomorrow as you are of their today.

❖

We are assembled here in the presence of God to celebrate and support the marriage of _____ and _____. They ask for your blessing, encouragement, and life long support for their decision to become husband and wife. They are delighted that you are here and thank you for your presence and participation on this special day.

❖

We are gathered here today in the sight of God, and the presence of friends and loved ones, to celebrate one of life's greatest moments. We are here to give recognition to the worth and beauty of love, and to add our best wishes and blessings to the words that will unite _____ and _____ in holy matrimony.

❖

_____ and _____ have invited you here today to share with them in this joyous celebration of their love and desire to join their lives together in marriage. We are here to rejoice and remember that it is love that leads us to our true destinations and to celebrate with _____ and _____ on their arrival in love and respect at this altar. We are here to celebrate the marriage of _____ and _____, to honor the beginning of their new life.

We're here to listen, to love, to dance and celebrate and to send them into their future with one outrageous, gigantic blessing. So sit back now, open your hearts, and let the wedding begin!

~ adapted from Weddings from the Heart, **Daphne Rose Kingma**

❖

Friends, family and members of the community, welcome to this ceremony, which will unite two souls in marriage.

❖

We have come here today, in the presence of God, to celebrate and support the choice of _____ and _____, to join in marriage. Love is a miraculous gift, and a wedding is a celebration of that magic, and that's why we are here today—to share in that magic!

❖

_____ and _____, today, in the presence of God, you are surrounded by your family and friends, all of whom are gathered to witness your exchange of vows and to share in the joy of this occasion. Let this be a statement of what you mean to each other, and the commitment of marriage that you will make.

❖

Non-spiritual Introductions

_____ and _____ want to welcome you to this celebration of their love for one another. Each of you has given something special to their lives. Your love and encouragement will forever be appreciated. Thank you for sharing one of life's happiest moments with them. May you be as important a part of their tomorrow as you are of their today.

❖

Welcome. A wedding is such a wonderful occasion, filled with hopes, dreams, and excitement. We are here today to celebrate the love that _____ and _____ have for each other, and to recognize and witness their decision to journey forward in their lives as marriage partners.

❖

_____ and _____ have asked all of you to be with them today because each of you has given something of yourself to their lives. Your friendship and love will always be appreciated. They welcome you here and thank you for sharing this important day with them.

❖

Marriage is a supreme sharing of experience, an adventure in the most intimate of human relationships. Today _____ and _____ proclaim their love and commitment to the world. We gather here to rejoice, with and for them, in the new life they now undertake together.

❖

_____ and _____ want to thank you for sharing with them this special and joyous day. Those of you, who have had the pleasure of spending some time with _____ and _____ have seen for yourselves that they possess a very rare and exceptional love. We are here today to celebrate their love and participate in this most wonderful occasion.

❖

We have come together for the marriage of ___ and ___.

❖

We have come here today to celebrate and support the choice of _____ and _____ to join in marriage. Love is a miraculous gift, and a wedding is a celebration of that magic, and that's why we are here today—to share in that magic!

❖

_____ and _____, today you are surrounded by your family and friends, all of whom are gathered to witness your exchange of vows and to share in the joy of this occasion. Let this be a statement of what you mean to each other and the commitment of marriage that you will make.

❖

Opening & Dedication Blessings

Spiritual Blessings

If I speak in the tongues of men and of angels, but have not love, I am only a resounding gong or a clanging cymbal. If I have the gift of prophecy and can fathom all mysteries and all knowledge, and if I have a faith that can move mountains, but have not love, I am nothing. If I give all I possess to the poor and surrender my body to the flames, but have not love, I gain nothing.

Love is patient, love is kind. It does not envy, it does not boast, it is not proud. It is not rude, it is not self-seeking, it is not easily angered, it keeps no record of wrongs. Love does not delight in evil but rejoices with the truth. It always protects, always trusts, always hopes, always perseveres.

Love never fails. But where there are prophecies, they will cease; where there are tongues, they will be stilled; where there is knowledge, it will pass away. For we know in part and we prophesy in part, but when perfection comes, the imperfect disappears.

When I was a child, I talked like a child, I thought like a child, I reasoned like a child. When I became a man, I put childish ways behind me. Now we see but a poor reflection as in a mirror; then we shall see face to face. Now I know in part; then I shall know fully, even as I am fully known. And now these three remain: faith, hope and love. But the greatest of these is love.

~ I Corinthians 13:1-13 (commonly known as the "love chapter" of the Bible)

Within this blessed union of souls, where two hearts intertwine to become one, there lies a promise. Perfectly born, divinely created, and intimately shared, it is a place where the hope and majesty of beginnings reside; where all things are made possible by the astounding love shared by two spirits. As you hold each other's hands in this promise, and eagerly look into the future in each other's eyes, may your unconditional love and devotion take you to places where you've both only dreamed. Where you'll dwell for a lifetime of happiness, sheltered in the warmth of each other's arms.

~ The Promise, **Heather Berry**

My beloved responded and said to me,
'Arise, my darling, my beautiful one,
And come along.
'For behold, the winter is past,
The rain is over and gone.
'The flowers have already appeared in the land;
The time has arrived for pruning the vines,
And the voice of the turtledove has been heard in our land.
'The fig tree has ripened its figs,
And the vines in blossom have given forth their fragrance.
Arise, my darling, my beautiful one,
And come along!'

~ Song of Solomon 2:10-13

You were born together, and together you shall be forevermore. You shall be together when the white wings of death scatter your days. Ay, you shall be together even in the silent memory of God. But let there be spaces in your togetherness, and let the winds of the heavens dance between you.

Love one another, but make not a bond of love: Let it rather be a moving sea between the shores of your souls. Fill each other's cup but drink not from one cup. Give one another of your bread but eat not from the same loaf. Sing and dance together and be joyous, but let each one of you be alone; Even as the strings of a lute are alone though they quiver with the same music.

Give your hearts, but not into each other's keeping. For only the hand of Life can contain your hearts. And stand together yet not too near together: For the pillars of the temple stand apart, and the oak tree and the cypress grow not in each other's shadow.

~ "On Marriage" from "The Prophet", **Kahlil Gibran**

Dear God, we pray for _____ and _____ as they enter into the sacred vows of marriage, that they may live according to their promises to each other and that they may create a marriage that is filled with joy and gentleness. We pray that as they enter into the deepest mysteries and wonders of love, that they are able to create a sanctuary in their hearts for each other.

❖

Dear Heavenly Father, we ask for your blessing today for _____ and _____, as they make these vows to each other to join together as one with You and each other. We pray for Your Holy Spirit to fill their hearts and their souls, and be the lamp that lights their paths throughout their commitment to an everlasting covenant. May this marriage be filled with Your love, as well as their love for each other. Amen.

~ Christopher Childers

❖

Dear Heavenly Father, We come to You, thanking you for this day and the decision that _____ and _____ are making to join each other in life. We pray that you would give them the strength and wisdom to take things as they come and persevere through the hard times and celebrate with each other in the good times. And we thank You that Your presence is here, that Your blessing would go throughout this day, that You would provide guidance not only during this ceremony but throughout their marriage. And the words that they speak today would ring true in their hearts for not only today but for the rest of their lives. In Jesus name, Amen.

~ Pastor Delane Hollstein

I add my breath to your breath
That our days may be long on the Earth,
That the days of our people may be long,
That we shall be as one person,
That we may finish our road together.

- Pueblo Blessing

God in heaven above please protect the ones we love.
We honor all you created as we pledge our hearts and lives together.
We honor mother-earth and ask for our marriage to be abundant
and grow stronger through the seasons;
We honor fire and ask that our union be warm and glowing with
love in our hearts;
We honor wind and ask that we sail though life safe and calm as in
our father's arms;
We honor water, to clean and soothe our relationship, that it may
never thirst for love;
With all the forces of the universe you created, we pray for harmony
and true happiness as we forever grow young together. Amen.

- Cherokee Prayer

May the words spoken here today and the choice of ____
and ____ to enter into this union, be filled with blessing. May their
marriage provide the love and support for each of them to expand
into their greatest purpose. May God continually guide their path
both individually, and as a couple. Amen.

May _____ and _____ continuously take delight in each
other and their marriage. And as they grow closer through the years,
may they also help each other grow closer to God. Amen.

May _____ and _____, surrender their relationship to God's loving purpose. May the joining together of their lives provide a sanctuary where they feel secure to explore both their individuality as well as who they are together. Amen.

Lord, make us instruments of your peace.
Where there is hatred, let us sow love;
Where there is injury, pardon;
Where there is discord, union;
Where there is doubt, faith;
Where there is despair, hope;
Where there is darkness, light;
Where there is sadness, joy;
O Divine Master, Grant that we may not so much seek
To be consoled as to console,
To be understood as to understand,
To be loved as to love.
For it is in giving that we receive;
It is in pardoning that we are pardoned;
And it is in dying that we are born to eternal life. Amen

~ *THE PRAYER,* **St. Francis of Assisi**

❖

1. We acknowledge the Unity of all within the sovereignty of God, expressing our appreciation for this wine, symbol and aid of our rejoicing.

2. We acknowledge the Unity of all within the sovereignty of God, realizing that each separate moment and every distinct object points to and shares in this oneness.

3. We acknowledge the Unity of all within the sovereignty of God, recognizing and appreciating the blessing of being human.

4. We acknowledge the Unity of all within the sovereignty of God, realizing the special gift of awareness that permits us to perceive this unity and the wonder we experience as a man and a woman joined to live together.

5. May rejoicing resound throughout the world as the homeless are given homes, persecution and oppression cease, and all people learn to live in peace with each other and in harmony with their environment.

6. From the Divine, source of all energy, we call forth an abundance of love to envelop this couple. May they be for each other lovers and friends, and may their love partake of the same innocence, purity, and sense of discovery that we imagine the first couple to have experienced.

7. We acknowledge the Unity of all within the sovereignty of God, and we highlight today joy and gladness, bridegroom and bride, delight and cheer, love and harmony, peace and companionship. May we all witness the day when the dominant sounds through the world will be these sounds of happiness, the voices of lovers, the sounds of feasting and singing.

~ *THE SEVEN BLESSINGS, From "The New Jewish Wedding", **Anita Diamant***

❖

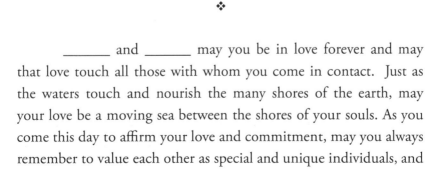

_____ and _____ may you be in love forever and may that love touch all those with whom you come in contact. Just as the waters touch and nourish the many shores of the earth, may your love be a moving sea between the shores of your souls. As you come this day to affirm your love and commitment, may you always remember to value each other as special and unique individuals, and may you respect each other's thoughts, ideas and feelings. May you be able to forgive and to forget and from this day forward may you be each other's home, comfort and sanctuary.

I would like at this time to speak of some things, which we pray for you. First, we pray for you a love that continues to give you joy and peace that provides you with energy to face the responsibilities of life. We pray for you a home of serenity. Not just a place of private joy and retreat, but a temple wherein the values of God and family are generated and upheld. Finally, we pray that as you grow together, you are able to look back at your lives together, and say these two things to each other: Because you loved me, you have given me faith in myself; because I have seen the good in you, I have received from you a faith in humanity.

Marriage is a very special place, the sheltered environment in which we can endlessly explore ourselves in the presence of another and in which we can offer the possibility of true reflection of another. May the vision that _____ and _____ have of one another, be always informed by the radiant force that first brought them together, and we pray that as they move into the sacredness of marriage that they always hold one another in the light of all light, and the love of all love.

- adapted from Weddings from the Heart, **Daphne Rose Kingma**

Enfolded in joy, inhabited by hope, bathed in the infinite spectrum of light that is love, may you always be infused with it and beautifully illuminated by it.

May every desire you have for your love be fulfilled. May your vision clearly behold one another. May you hear each other most genuinely. And may you give of your endless generosity of spirit to nourish one another's soul and sweetly keep the promises you make here today.

- adapted from Weddings from the Heart, **Daphne Rose Kingma**

❖

Non-spiritual Wishes

Joy, gentle friends! Joy and fresh days of love accompany your hearts!

- William Shakespeare

❖

Now join your hands, and with your hands your hearts.

- William Shakespeare

❖

Inspired by their love, let each of us rededicate ourselves to the loving relationships in our own lives. May we all be enriched for having shared this day together.

❖

_____ and _____, through your marriage, and through your love, may you give the gifts of tenderness, comfort, joy, and peace to each other to nurture you throughout the years.

❖

Let my love, like sunshine, surround you, and illuminate your freedom.

- Tagore

❖

Greet each day with your eyes open to beauty, your mind open to change, and your heart open to love.

~ Paula Finn

I would like at this time to speak of some things, which we wish for you. First, we wish for you a love that continues to give you joy and peace that provides you with energy to face the responsibilities of life. We wish for you a home of serenity. Not just a place of private joy and retreat, but a temple wherein the values of family are generated and upheld. Finally, we wish that as you grow together, you are able to look back at your lives together and say these two things to each other: Because you loved me, you have given me faith in myself; because I have seen the good in you, I have received from you a faith in humanity.

May your fulfillment and joy in each other and in yourselves increase with every passing year. And, may you continue to deepen your life with each other and with all conscious beings.

Marriage is a very special place, the sheltered environment in which we can endlessly explore ourselves in the presence of another and in which we can offer the possibility of true reflection of another. May the vision that _____ and _____ have of one another be always informed by the radiant force that first brought them together, and we wish that as they move into the commitment of marriage that they always hold one another in the love of all love.

~ adapted from Weddings from the Heart, **Daphne Rose Kingma**

May every desire you have for your love be fulfilled. May your vision clearly behold one another. May you hear each other most genuinely. And may you give of your endless generosity to nourish one another's hearts and sweetly keep the promises you make here today.

- adapted from Weddings from the Heart, **Daphne Rose Kingma**

Marriage is a place of freedom. Freedom to fully express who you are, knowing that you have someone there to catch you when you fall, encourage you when you are discouraged, and applaud your successes. May the life you choose to share, lavishly fulfill each of you, inspiring you to give abundantly to the rest of the world. May the promises you make here today, reflect the love and sincerity of your truest intention for this union. When life is peaceful and when it is painful, may you continuously be reminded of the beauty and deepest intention of the vows you make here today.

Addresses

Spiritual Addresses

_____ and _____, marriage is the most important of all human relationships. It should be entered into reverently, thoughtfully and with full understanding of its sacred nature. Your marriage must stand by the strength of your love and the power of faith in each other and in God. Just as two threads woven in opposite directions form a beautiful tapestry, so too your lives when merged together will make a beautiful marriage. It is a mutual enrichment; a mingling of two personalities which diminishes neither, and enhances both. Marriage is a fusion of two hearts, the union of two lives, the coming together of two rivers, which after being united in marriage, will flow in the same channel in the same direction. To make your relationship succeed will take love. This is the core of your marriage and why you are here today. It will take trust, to know in your hearts that you truly want the best for each other. It will take dedication, to stay open and honest with one another and to learn and grow together. It will take faith, to go forward together without knowing exactly what the future brings. And it will take commitment to hold true to the journey you both promise today to share together. An intimate and secure relationship is not based solely on promises, but also on trust, respect, faithfulness and the ability to forgive. A lasting marriage is based on all of these, bound together by love.

_____ and _____, today you are affirming before witnesses of earth and heaven that you believe God has intended that you should share life in the holy union of matrimony. Your marriage must stand by the strength of your love and the power of faith in each other and in God. There is no relationship on earth as intimate or meaningful as those you are about to enter. There is no human institution more sacred than that of the home you are about to form. The life that each of you have experienced up until now, individually, will hereafter be inseparably united. Spiritual marriage is based on this deep, invisible union of two souls who seek to find completion in one another. A cord of three strands is not easily broken, so too your lives when merged together with Spirit will create a beautiful marriage that is strengthened by God's love. This is the core of your marriage and why you are here today. It will take trust, to know in your hearts that you truly want the best for each other. It will take dedication, to stay open and honest with one another and to learn and grow together. It will take faith, to go forward together without knowing exactly what the future brings. And it will take commitment to hold true to the journey you both promise today to share together. An intimate and secure relationship is not based solely on promises, but also on trust, respect, faithfulness and the ability to forgive. A lasting marriage is based on all of these, bound together by love.

A spiritual relationship is formed when two (or more) people come together, as equals, for the purpose of spiritual growth. Within a Spiritual Relationship, both parties agree that nothing is more important than their spiritual evolution. Spiritual relationships create a synergy, which enables each partner to spiritually evolve faster than they could alone. This divine energy is what I believe Jesus was referring to when he said, "Where two or more are gathered in my name!"

Spiritual Partners commit to a growing dynamic. Their commitment is truly a promise toward their own spiritual growth and enhancement, and not to their physical survival.

~ Gary Zukav

Your love requires space in which to grow. This space must be safe enough to allow your hearts to be revealed. It must offer refreshment for your spirits and renewal for your minds. It must be a space made sacred by the quality of your honesty, attention, love and compassion.

~ A Sacred Space, **Lau Tzu**

Nothing happens without a cause. The union of this man and woman has not come about accidentally but is the foreordained result of many past lives. This tie can therefore not be broken or dissolved.

~ Buddhist Marriage Homily

Marriage is an Athenic weaving together of families, of two souls with their individual fates and destinies, of time and eternity—everyday life married to the timeless mysteries of the soul.

~ Thomas Moore

The most wonderful of all things in life, I believe, is the discovery of another human being with whom one's relationship has a growing depth, beauty, and joy as the years increase. This inner progressiveness of love between two human beings is a most marvelous thing, it cannot be found by looking for it or by passionately wishing for it. It is sort of a Divine accident.

~ The Most Wonderful of All Things in Life, **Sir Hugh Walpole**

Marriage symbolizes the ultimate intimacy between a man and a woman, yet this closeness should not diminish but strengthen the individuality of each partner. A marriage that lasts is one that always has a little more to grow. It is out of the resonance between individuality and union that love, whose incredible strength is equal only to its incredible fragility, is born and reborn.

Marriage is a lifetime commitment, which recognizes the negative as well as the positive aspects of life.

Marriage's content is never predetermined. It is a living organism that reflects the continuous choices of the individuals involved.

In marrying we promise to love not only as we feel right now, but also as we intend to feel. In marriage we say not only, "I love you today," but also, "I promise to love you tomorrow, the next day and always."

Love doesn't limit. Love brings with it the gift of freedom. Love teaches us to encourage the people we love to make their own choices, seek their own path and learn their lessons in their own way and in their own time. Love also teaches us to share our feelings and thoughts with each other about those choices. We can then make decisions openly and freely, through our love, which allows both to grow. Love that restrains is not love. To restrain another in the name of love, doesn't create love, it creates restraint.

Love means each person is free to follow his or her own heart. If we truly love, our choices will naturally and freely serve that love well. When we give freedom to another, we really give freedom to ourselves.

In promising always, we promise each other time. We promise to exercise our love, to stretch it large enough to embrace the unforeseen realities of the future. We promise to learn to love beyond the level of our instincts and inclinations, to love in hard times as well as when we are exhilarated by the pleasures of romance.

We change because of these promises. We shape ourselves according to them; we live in their midst and live differently because of them. We feel protected because of them. We try some things and resist trying others because, having promised, we feel secure—to see, to be, to love. Our souls are protected; our hearts have come home.

When we are safe in marriage, we can risk. Because we know we are loved, we can step beyond our fears; because we have chosen, we can transcend our insecurities. We can make mistakes, knowing we will not be cast out; take missteps, knowing someone will be there to catch us. And because mistakes and missteps are the stuff of change, of expansion, in marriage we can expand to our fullest capacity.

So remember these things, as you go out into the world as a couple: that your love will have seasons, that your relationship is a progression, and that love will prevail. Remembering each other, holding each other in your hearts and your minds, will give you a marriage as deep in its joy, as your courtship has been in its magic.

Congratulations _____ and _____, the real fun has just begun.

~ adapted from Weddings from the Heart, **Daphne Rose Kingma**

❖

Marriage is a commitment, which should not be entered into lightly. It is the union of two souls, two hearts and two minds. The Celtic belief of the soul is that it exists within and outside the individual; it is manifest in the trees, the rocks, the waters and the Sun. The relationship between humans and the world around them is intertwined. The soul is inextricably tied to the universal spirit of the Earth.

Non-spiritual Addresses

It is only through your relationship with people, places and events that you can even exist. The purpose of a relationship is to decide what part of yourself you'd like to see "show up," not what part of another you can capture and hold. The purpose of relationships is not to have another who might complete you; but to have another with whom you might share your completeness.

~ Neale Donald Walsch

A soulmate is someone who has locks that fit our keys, and keys to fit our locks. When we feel safe enough to open the locks, our truest selves step out and we can be completely and honestly who we are; we can be loved for who we are and not for who we're pretending to be. Each unveils the best part of the other. No matter what else goes wrong around us, with that one person we're safe in our own paradise.

Our soulmate is someone who shares our deepest longings, our sense of direction. When we're two balloons, and together our direction is up, chances are we've found the right person. Our soulmate is the one who makes life come to life.

~ Excerpt from The Bridge Across Forever, **Richard Bach**

Marriage is a commitment to life, the best that two people can find and bring out in each other. It offers opportunities for sharing and growth that no other relationship can equal. It is a physical and an emotional joining that is promised for a lifetime.

Within the circle of its love, marriage encompasses all of life's most important relationships. A wife and a husband are each other's best friend, confidant, lover, teacher, listener, and critic. And there may come times when one partner is heartbroken or ailing, and the love of the other may resemble the tender caring of a parent for a child.

Marriage deepens and enriches every facet of life. Happiness is fuller, memories are fresher, commitment is stronger, even anger is felt more strongly, and passes away more quickly.

Marriage understands and forgives the mistakes life is unable to avoid. It encourages and nurtures new life, new experiences, and new ways of expressing a love that is deeper than life.

When two people pledge their love and care for each other in marriage, they create a spirit unique unto themselves which binds them closer than any spoken or written words. Marriage is a promise, a potential made in the hearts of two people who love each other and takes a lifetime to fulfill.

~ Marriage Joins Two People in the Circle of its Love, **Edmund O'Neill**

When you love someone, you do not love them all the time, in exactly the same way, from moment to moment. It is an impossibility. It is even a lie to pretend to. And yet this is exactly what most of us demand. We have so little faith in the ebb and flow of life, of love, of relationships. We leap at the flow of the tide and resist in terror its ebb. We are afraid it will never return.

We insist on permanency, on duration, on continuity; when the only continuity possible, in life as in love, is in growth, in fluidity—in freedom, in the sense that the dancers are free, barely touching as they pass, but partners in the same pattern.

The only real security is not in owning or possessing, not in demanding or expecting, not in hoping, even. Security in a relationship lies neither in looking back to what was in nostalgia, nor forward to what it might be in dread or anticipation, but living in the present relationship and accepting it as it is now.

Relationships must be like islands, one must accept them for what they are here and now, within their limits—islands, surrounded and interrupted by the sea, and continually visited and abandoned by the tides.

- From "Gift from the Sea", **Anne Morrow Lindbergh**

You can give without loving,
but you can never love without giving.
The great acts of love are done by those
who are habitually performing small acts of kindness.
We pardon to the extent that we love.
Love is knowing that even when you are alone,
you will never be lonely again.
And great happiness of life is the conviction that we are loved.
Loved for ourselves.
And even loved in spite of ourselves.

- Author Unknown

The little things are the big things. It is never being too old to hold hands. It is remembering to say "I love you" at least once a day.

It is never going to sleep angry. It is at no time taking the other for granted; the courtship should not end with the honeymoon, it should continue through all the years.

It is having a mutual sense of values and common objectives. It is standing together facing the world. It is forming a circle of love that gathers in the whole family. It is doing things for each other, not in the attitude of duty or sacrifice, but in the spirit of joy.

It is speaking words of appreciation and demonstrating gratitude in thoughtful ways. It is not expecting the husband to wear a halo or the wife to have wings of an angel. It is not looking for perfection in each other.

It is cultivating flexibility, patience, understanding and a sense of humor. It is having the capacity to forgive and forget. It is giving each other an atmosphere in which each can grow.

It is finding room for the things of the spirit. It is a common search for the good and the beautiful. It is establishing a relationship in which the independence is equal, dependence is mutual and the obligation is reciprocal. It is not only marrying the right partner, it is being the right partner.

- The Art of Marriage, **Wilfred A. Peterson**

When we feel safe in the presence of our loved one, there is no need to hide any part of ourselves for fear of being judged or rejected. There is a gentleness to the presence of love that softens life's rough edges. It makes us braver to go forth into the world knowing that the shelter of someone's love awaits us at the end of the day. And in choosing to share ourselves with another, we trust that our lives will be far richer than had we chosen separate journeys through this world.

Couples, who nourish a strong and enduring love, sustain long lasting relationships. They create space in the relationship for both of them to be unique individuals. They are able to express themselves without fear of being judged or rejected. They are free to surrender, to be vulnerable, and to be known and loved without condition.

The meaning of marriage begins in the giving of words. We cannot join ourselves to one another without giving our word. And this must be an unconditional giving, for in joining ourselves to one another we join ourselves to the unknown ... You do not know the road; you have committed your life to the way.

~ Ralph Waldo Emerson

❖

No distance of place or lapse of time can lessen the love of those who are thoroughly persuaded of each other's worth.

~ Robert Southey

❖

Love is that condition in which the happiness of another person is essential to your own.

~ Robert A. Heinlein

❖

Oh, the comfort, the inexpressible comfort of feeling safe with a person; having neither to weigh thoughts nor measure words, but to pour them all out, chaff and grain together, knowing that a faithful hand will take and sift them, keep what is worth keeping; and then, with the breath of kindness, blow the rest away.

~ Dinah Maria Mulock Craik

❖

The question is asked, "Is there anything more beautiful in life than a young couple clasping hands and pure hearts in the path of marriage? Can there be anything more beautiful than young love?" And the answer is given. "Yes, there is a more beautiful thing. It is the spectacle of an old man and an old woman finishing their journey together on that path. Their hands are gnarled, but still clasped; their faces are seamed, but still radiant; their hearts are physically bowed and tired, but still strong with love and devotion for one another. Yes, there is a more beautiful thing than young love. Old love."

~ Author Unknown

_____ and _____ the relationship that you have nurtured together stands for love that will blossom and grow with each passing day. Before you knew love, you were friends, and it was from this seed of friendship that is now your destiny. Marriage is the clasping of hands, the blending of hearts, the union of two lives as one. Marriage is caring as much about the welfare and happiness of your marriage partner as your own, it is not total absorption into each other; it is looking outward in the same direction together. Marriage makes burdens lighter because you divide them. It makes joys more intense because you share them. It makes you stronger, so you can be involved with life in ways you dare not risk alone. To make your relationship succeed will take love. This is the core of your marriage and why you are here today. It will take trust, to know in your hearts that you truly want the best for each other. It will take dedication, to stay open and honest with one another—and to learn and grow together. It will take faith, to go forward together without knowing exactly what the future brings. And it will take commitment, to hold true to the journey you both will promise today to share together. An intimate and secure relationship is not based solely on promises, but also on trust, respect, faithfulness and the ability to forgive. A lasting marriage is based on all of these, bound together by love.

~ Author Unknown

As you know, no one person can marry you. Only you can marry yourselves. By a mutual commitment to love each other, to work toward creating an atmosphere of care, consideration and respect, by a willingness to face life's anxieties together, you can make your wedded life your strength. On this day of your wedding you stand somewhat apart from other people. You stand within the light of your love; and this is as it should be. You will experience a lot together, some wonderful, some difficult. But even when it is difficult you must manage to call upon the strength in the love you have for each other to see you through. From this day onward you must come closer together than ever before, you must love one another with the strength that makes this bond a marriage. As you exchange your vows, remember that the sensual part of love is great, but when this is combined with real friendship both are infinitely enhanced.

_____ and _____, you are about to take a new step forward into life. Courtesy and consideration, even in anger and adversity, are the seeds of compassion. Love is the fruit of compassion. Trust, love, and respect are the sustaining virtues of marriage. They enable us to learn from each situation, and help us to realize that everywhere we turn we meet our Self.

We nourish ourselves and each other in living by the following five principles:

1. In every way we can, we allow our deepest Self to appear.
2. We take full responsibility for our own life, in all its infinite dimensions.
3. We trust in the honesty and wisdom of our own essence, which with our love and reverence always shows us the true way.
4. We embrace all parts of our Self, including our deepest fears and shadows, so that they may be transformed.
5. We are willing to keep our heart open, even in the midst of great pain.

Declaration of Intent

Spiritual Declarations

_____, do you take _____ as your (husband/wife/partner), joining with (him/her) today in spirit, offering your friendship and loving care? Do you promise to honor (his/her) growth and freedom as well as your own, to cherish and respect (him/her), to love and embrace (him/her) in times of challenge as well as times of joy? [I do]

❖

_____, do you promise, _____, before God, your family and friends, to commit your love to _____; to respect (his/her) individuality; to be with (him/her) through life's changes; and to nurture and strengthen the love between you, as long as you both shall live? [I do]

❖

_____, do you take _____, as your (wife/husband). Do you promise, in the presence of God, to love and cherish (him/her), to grow with (him/her), and to have faith in your journey together through all the changes that will come? Do you promise to share your life and all that you are with (him/her)? [I do]

❖

_____, do you promise, _____, in the presence of God, that you will love (him/her) for today and for all of your tomorrows. And that from this day forward, you will walk beside (him/her)? [I do]

❖

_____, do you promise, _____, in the presence of God, that you will stand by (him/her) always? Do you promise to have faith in (him/her) and encourage (him/her)? Do you promise to be there to listen to (him/her), to laugh with (him/her), and to hold (him/her)? Will you work with (him/her) as you build a life together, and support (him/her) as you live your own independent life? Will you strive every day, to make your relationship stronger? And do you promise to be (his/her) friend, (his/her) love, and (his/her) partner for all the days of your lives? [I do]

❖

_____, do you vow to ____, in the presence of God, that every day, you will hold your marriage sacred, and appreciate (him/her) as the greatest gift of your life? [I do]

❖

____, do you vow, before God, your families and friends, to always be there for ____. To help (him/her) with tough decisions and to always share your feelings. To support (his/her) dreams and to shelter (him/her) when times are difficult. To apologize, forgive and work to resolve misunderstandings. To trust (him/her) and to always believe in (him/her). To faithfully love (him/her) forever, with all of your heart? [I do]

❖

Non-spiritual Declarations

_____, do you take _____ as your (husband/wife/partner), joining with (him/her) today in marriage, offering your friendship and loving care? Do you promise to honor (his/her) growth and freedom as well as your own, to cherish and respect (him/her), to love and embrace (him/her) in times of challenge as well as times of joy? [I do]

❖

_____, will you (embrace/take) _____ as your (wife/husband)? As your companion and best friend for life, will you treat (her/him) with love and devotion, honor and respect? Will you stand by (her/him) in the triumphs and tragedies of life, as a faithful and caring (wife/husband)? [I Will]

❖

_____, do you (receive/embrace/take) _____, to be your (wife/husband)? Do you promise to love, adore, and encourage (her/him)? Share the good times and achievements as well as the hard times and disappointments? Keep (her/him) in sickness and in sorrow and to be loyal to (her/him) forevermore? [I do]

❖

_____, will you take this (woman/man) whose hand you now hold, choosing (him/her) alone to be your (husband/wife)? Will you love (her/him), comfort (her/him), showing kindness, understanding and respect throughout your lives? [I will]

❖

_____, do you give yourself totally to loving _____, striving to do whatever you can to help (her/him) feel content and secure, treating (her/him) with affection, understanding and admiration throughout your life together? [I do]

❖

_____, do you take _____, to be your (wife/husband), to love, honor, comfort and cherish, from this day forward? [I do]

❖

_____ and _____, do you choose to enter into this marriage believing the love you share and your faith in each other will endure all things? [We do]

❖

_____, do you (receive/embrace/take) _____, to be your (wife/husband)? Do you promise to love (her/him), respect (her/him) and care for (her/him), under all conditions and circumstances of life, to be a faithful (wife/husband) to (her/him) for the rest of your lives together? [I do]

❖

____, do you now choose, ____ to be your life companion, to share your life openly with (him/her), to speak truthfully and lovingly to (him/her), to accept (him/her) fully as (he/she) is and delight in who (he/she) is becoming; to respect (his/her) uniqueness, encourage (his/her) fulfillment, and compassionately support (him/her) through all the changes of your years together? [I do]

❖

____, do you give your promise, that from this day forward, ____ shall never walk alone. That your heart will be (his/her) shelter, your arms will be (his/her) home. Do you promise to walk together through life as partners and best friends, and that you shall always do your best to love and accept ____ exactly the way (he/she) is. Do you give (him/her) freedom and your trust, and do you give your heart until the end of time? [I do]

❖

_____, do you take, _____, to have and to hold from this day forward, for better for worse, for richer for poorer, in sickness and in health, to love and to cherish, till death do you part? [I do]

- Traditional Vows

❖

_____, do you promise, _____, to be (his/her) friend, to comfort and listen to (him/her). To celebrate (his/her) successes and to support (his/her) struggles. To love, respect, and tenderly care for (him/her), through all the days of your life? [I do]

- (adapted) **Andrea L. Mack**

❖

_____, do you choose, _____, this day, to love and confide in, to hold on to and reach out from, to believe in and to share with, to learn from and grow with? Do you choose, this day, to give (him/her) your heart? [I do]

- (adapted) **Rabbi Rami M. Shapiro**

❖

_____, do you promise, _____, before your family and friends, to commit your love to _____; to respect (his/her) individuality; to be with (him/her) through life's changes; and to nurture and strengthen the love between you, as long as you both shall live? [I do]

❖

_____, do you take _____, as your (wife/husband). Do you promise to love and cherish (him/her), to grow with (him/her), and to have faith in your journey together through all the changes that will come? Do you promise to share your life and all that you are with (him/her)? [I do]

❖

_____, do you promise, ____, that you will love (him/her) for today and for all of your tomorrows? And that from this day forward, you will walk beside (him/her)? [I do]

❖

_____, do you promise, ____, that you will stand by (him/her) always? Do you promise to have faith in (him/her) and encourage (him/her)? Do you promise to be there to listen to (him/her), to laugh with (him/her), and to hold (him/her)? Will you work with (him/her) as you build a life together, and support (him/her) as you live your own independent life? Will you strive every day, to make your relationship stronger? And do you promise to be (his/her) friend, (his/her) love, and (his/her) partner for all the days of your lives? [I do]

❖

_____, do you vow to ____, that every day, you will hold your marriage sacred, and appreciate (him/her) as the greatest gift of your life? [I do]

❖

____, do you vow to always be there for ____,
To help (him/her) with tough decisions and to always share your feelings,
To support (his/her) dreams and to shelter (him/her) when times are difficult,
To apologize, forgive and work to resolve misunderstandings,
To trust (him/her) and to always believe in (him/her),
To faithfully love (him/her) forever, with all of your heart? [I do]

❖

_____, do you promise _____, that from this day onward you will stand with (him/her) in sickness and health, in joy and sorrow, and do you pledge to (him/her) your respect and your love? [I do]

❖

_____ and _____, you have declared your intention to make this venture of faith and love, realizing that from this time forward your destinies will be woven of one design and your challenges and joys will be shared together. Today you are making public, before family and friends, that the words, "I love you," are a full commitment of yourselves, one to the other.

Understanding that marriage is the convergence of your individual and joint destinies as well as the greatest support for them,

_____, do you choose to marry, _____, and have her as your wife? [I do]

_____, do you choose to marry, _____, and have him as your husband? [I do]

~ adapted from Weddings from the Heart, **Daphne Rose Kingma**

The Vows

Spiritual Vows

I have found the one whom my soul loves.

~ Song of Solomon 3:4

My heart can be your home. My soul can be your refuge. You can turn to me when you are weak. You can call to me when the way is not clear.

I will be your promise, your prayer, and I will always be there, constant, complete. Run to me, reach out for me and I will love you in a unique and tender way. Bring your love to me. Share your love with me. Sing your love to me, and I will give you peace, ease and comfort.

*~ **Lori Eberhardy***

_____, you are my companion in life and my one true love. I will treasure our friendship and love you today, tomorrow, and forever. I will trust and honor you. I will laugh and cry with you. With unfailing love I will stand by you, through the best and the worst, through the difficult and the easy. As I have given you my hand to hold, so I give you my life to keep, so help me God.

❖

I _____, (receive/take) you _____, as my wedded (wife/husband), to have and to hold, from this day forward, for better, for worse, for richer, for poorer, in sickness and in health, to love and to cherish, till death us do part; according to God's holy will.

❖

_____, I take you to be my (husband/wife), I promise to be faithful to you and honest with you; I will respect, help and care for you; I will share my life with you; I will forgive you as we have been forgiven; and I will try with you to better understand ourselves, the world, and God; through the best and the worst as long as we live.

❖

My Soulmate, you know my heart as I know yours. Let us be gentle with each other's emotions and patient with each other's frailties. And let us face what life brings us, with grace and love.

~ Reverend Edie Weinstein-Moser

❖

_____, in finding you, my dreams have come true. In your love, I have found a home for my heart and soul.

❖

I, _____, take you, _____, to be my (husband/wife), my constant friend, my faithful partner and the love of my life. In the presence of God, our families and friends, I promise to be your faithful partner in sickness and in health, in good times and in bad, in happiness as well as in sadness. I promise to love you unconditionally, to support you in your aspirations, and to honor and respect you. This is my solemn vow.

❖

_____, today we begin our lives together.
I promise before God, our families and our friends
to be your faithful (husband/wife).
I choose to live with you, as your lover, companion and friend,
loving you when life is peaceful, and when it is painful,
during our successes, and during our failures,
supported by your strengths, and accepting your weaknesses.
I will honor your goals and dreams,
trying always, to encourage your fulfillment.
I will strive to be honest, and open with you,
sharing my thoughts, and my life with you.
I promise to love and cherish you
from this day forward.

❖

I choose you, _____,
To be my (wife/husband), from this time forward.
To love you, and be faithful to you,
To be a comfort, in your life,
To nourish you, with my gentleness,
To uphold you, with my strength,
To love your body, as it ages,

To weigh the effects, of the words I speak
And of the things I do,
To never take you for granted,
But always give thanks, for your presence.
I promise you this, from my heart,
With my soul,
For all the days of my life.

~ adapted from Weddings from the Heart, **Daphne Rose Kingma**

❖

I, _____, take you, _____ as my (wife/husband) and vow to be mindful in our journey together, to love you and to cherish you, to trust in the Universal soul, to have belief in my heart and faith in my mind. From this day forward our souls will be as one.

❖

Non-spiritual Vows

_____, I (embrace/receive) you this day to be my (wife/husband). I will have no greater love than you. I promise to stand by you in happiness and adversity, in riches or poverty, in sickness or health. I promise in faithfulness, to love and respect you and our marriage, for all my tomorrows and beyond.

❖

_____, I (embrace/receive) you, today as my (wife/husband). I will be true to you in all things. I will share what I have and who I am. I will stay with you in heartache, celebrate life with you in joy and receive you as my equal.

❖

_____, as your (wife/husband) and best friend I promise to love and encourage you; sharing hopes, dreams and secrets. I promise to be open and honest with you, caring for you in a lifelong commitment.

❖

I _____, (receive/take) you, _____, to be my (wife/husband). I will share the good times and hard times by your side. I give you my hand and my heart as a sanctuary of warmth and peace, and promise my faith and love to you, till the end of time.

❖

_____, I promise to love you, to be your best friend, to respect and support you, to be patient with you, to work together with you to achieve our goals, to accept you unconditionally and to share life with you throughout our years together.

❖

I promise to walk together through life as partners and best friends. I promise that I will always do my best to love and accept you exactly the way you are. I give you your freedom and my trust in you. I give you my heart until the end of time.

❖

I, _____, take you, _____, to have and to hold from this day forward, for better for worse, for richer for poorer, in sickness and in health, to love and to cherish, till death do us part.

- Traditional Vows

❖

From this day forward, you shall not walk alone.
My heart will be your shelter,
And my arms will be your home.

- **Author Unknown**

❖

I promise to be your friend, to comfort you, and listen to you.
To celebrate your successes, and to support your struggles.
To love you, respect you and tenderly care for you,
Through all the day of our lives.

~ Andrea L. Mack

I choose you this day to love and confide in,
To hold on to and reach out from.
I choose you this day to believe in and to share with,
To learn from and grow with.
I choose you this day to give you my heart.

~ Rabbi Rami M. Shapiro

_____, I promise, before family and friends, to commit my love to you; to respect your individuality; to be with you through life's changes; and to nurture and strengthen the love between us, as long as we both shall live.

_____, I take you, as my (wife/husband). I promise to love and cherish you, to grow with you, and to have faith in our journey together through all the changes that will come. I promise to share my life and all that I am with you.

_____, I will love you for today and for all of our tomorrows. From this day forward, I will walk beside you.

_____, you are my best friend. You are my precious love. You are the one I choose to spend my life with.

❖

_____, I will stand by you always. I will have faith in you and encourage you. I will be here to listen to you, to laugh with you, and to hold you. I will work with you as we build a life together, and support you as you live your own independent life. I will strive every day, to make our relationship stronger. I will be your friend, your love, and your partner for all the days of our lives.

❖

_____, I vow to you that every day, I will hold this marriage sacred, for you are the greatest gift of my life.

❖

_____, I promise, to respect you as an individual, with interests, desires, and needs as important as my own. To be your partner in celebrating our successes and facing our challenges. To be a loving (husband/wife) to you, and contribute daily to the health, comfort, and balance of our relationship. I promise to keep myself open to you, and to continuously delight in the privilege of sharing my life with you.

❖

I vow to always be here for you,
To help you with tough decisions,
and to always share my feelings,
To support your dreams
and to shelter you when times are difficult,
To apologize, forgive and work to resolve misunderstandings,
To trust you and to always believe in you,
To faithfully love you forever, with all of my heart.

❖

_____, today we begin our lives together. I promise before our families and our friends to be your faithful (husband/wife). I choose to live with you, as your lover, companion and friend, loving you when life is peaceful, and when it is painful, during our successes, and during our failures, supported by your strengths, and accepting your weaknesses. I will honor your goals and dreams, trying always, to encourage your fulfillment. I will strive to be honest, and open with you, sharing my thoughts, and my life with you. I promise to love and cherish you from this day forward.

❖

I, ___, take you, ___, to be my (husband/wife), in equal love, as a mirror for my true Self, as a partner on my path, to honor and to cherish, in sorrow and in joy, till death do us part.

❖

Blessing of the Rings

Spiritual Ring Blessings

These circles of precious metal are regarded as a symbol of the purity and eternity of the state of marriage. The ancients were reminded by the circle of eternity, as it is designed to have neither beginning nor end; while (gold/platinum) is so incorruptible that it cannot be tarnished by use or time. So may this union, be incorruptible in its purity and more lasting than time itself.

❖

The wedding ring is a symbol of unbroken unity. It portrays completeness and eternity. May the imperishable substance of these rings reflect a love shining with increasing radiance throughout your years together. May God bless these rings, which you give to each other as the sign of your love, trust, and devotion.

These rings are a sign and symbol of the vows _____ and _____ have made to one another. Lord bless these rings, that _____ and _____ exchange and wear as a sign of the covenant between them, may they ever remain in your peace, living together in unity, in love, and in happiness, desiring to do Your will.

❖

Let these rings symbolize the devotion and commitment each holds for the other. These rings, given in love, are an affirmation to all that bear witness that _____ and _____ are truly (joined/united) together as husband and wife. May God bless your union with His never-ending bond of love and peace.

❖

The wedding ring is the outward and visible sign of an inward and spiritual bond, which unites two souls in endless love. The perfect circle of a ring symbolizes eternity, while gold is a symbol of all that is pure and holy. As you give these rings to each other, our prayer is that your love will be the same; pure and eternal. St. Augustine said, "The nature of God is like a circle whose center is everywhere and circumference cannot be found." May these rings symbolize the nature of God in your lives.

❖

A circle is the symbol of the sun and the earth and the universe. It is a symbol of holiness and of perfection and of peace. In these rings it is the symbol of unity, in which your lives are now joined in one unbroken circle, in which, wherever you go, you will always return to your shared life together.

❖

These rings are an outward and visible sign of an inward and spiritual grace, signifying to all the uniting of _____ and _____ in the bond of matrimony. In the presence of God and these friends, seal your promises with rings, the symbol of the life you share together.

❖

The marriage ring seals the vows of marriage and represents a promise for eternal and everlasting love. It is a physical manifestation of the promises joining the bride and groom together. The wedding ring is placed on the fourth finger of the left hand because it was traditionally believed that this finger was a direct connection to the heart—the perfect place for a symbol representing eternal love and commitment.

❖

Through the exchange of these rings, with God's blessing, your commitment is sealed.

❖

Non-spiritual Ring Wishes

Words are powerful, but fleeting, and the sound of them is soon gone. Therefore, the wedding ring becomes the enduring symbol of the promises we have just heard.

❖

Through the exchange of these rings your commitment is sealed.

❖

The ring is a symbol of the unbroken circle of love. Love freely given has no beginning and no end, no giver and no receiver for each is the giver and each is the receiver. May these rings always remind you of the vows you have taken.

❖

Above all rings the wedding ring denotes purity, loyalty and grace. It is made of the purest metal to speak of the purity of marriage and is made in a circle to note the unending commitment you are about to enter.

❖

The marriage ring seals the vows of marriage and represents a promise for everlasting love. It is a physical manifestation of the promises joining the bride and groom together. The wedding ring is placed on the fourth finger of the left hand because it was traditionally believed that this finger was a direct connection to the heart—the perfect place for a symbol representing everlasting love and commitment.

❖

The ring, a circle, is one of nature's simplest forms. The arc of the rainbow, the halo of the moon and the smallest of raindrops simulate the circle. When a stone is cast upon a pond, it generates waves in ever expanding circles. Consider this marriage as being two stones striking the water simultaneously. The ensuing waves interlock, and the growth of the enlarging circles show the combined energies of the lives of _____ and _____. The interlocking of these two lives will be symbolized in the exchange of rings.

❖

These circles of precious metal are regarded as a symbol of the purity and timelessness of the state of Marriage. The ancients were reminded by the circle of infinity, as it is designed to have neither beginning nor end; while (gold/platinum) is so incorruptible that it cannot be tarnished by use or time. So may this union, be incorruptible in its purity and more lasting than time itself.

❖

And now, seal your promises with these rings, the symbol of the life you share together.

❖

These rings are an outward and visible sign of an inward and loving honor, signifying to all the uniting of _____ and _____ in the bond of matrimony. In the presence of these friends, seal your promises with rings, the symbol of the life you share together.

❖

Rings are made precious by our wearing them. The rings you exchange at your wedding are the most special because they say that even in your uniqueness you have chosen to share your lives, to allow the presence of another human being to enhance who you are. As you wear them through time, they will reflect not only who you are, but also what you have created together.

❖

Now _____ and _____ celebrate their love and proclaim their union with rings of precious metal. The precious nature of their rings represents the subtle and wonderful essence they find individually, through their mutual love, respect, and support. The metal itself represents the long life they may cultivate together, not only in years, but in all the infinite dimensions of each moment they share.

❖

Exchanging of the Rings

Spiritual Ring Exchanges

_____, I give you this ring as a symbol of my love. As it encircles your finger, may it remind you always that you are surrounded by my eternal love. Whenever you look at it, may it remind you of the vows we make today.

❖

This ring has no beginning and no ending, which symbolizes that the love between us is eternal. I place it on your finger as a visible sign of the vows, which have made us husband and wife.

❖

I give you this ring, as a symbol of my love, and as a reminder that our souls are now joined in a lifelong commitment.

With this ring I offer you my heart and soul. May its presence on your hand be a constant reminder of my love.

I give you this ring as a symbol of our vows, and with all that I am, and all that I have, I honor you, in the name of God.

_____, in token and (pledge/promise) of our faith and abiding love, with this ring I thee wed. In the name of the Father and of the Son and of the Holy Spirit. Amen.

Just as this ring is without end, so my love for you is eternal. Just as it is made of imperishable substance, my commitment to you will never fail. With this ring, I thee wed.

I offer you this ring, shaped as a symbol of completeness and eternity. Please wear this ring as a sign of our love and as a reminder of the promises we have made today.

I give you this ring as a sign of my devotion and love and with all my heart I promise to you, all that I am. With this ring I marry you and join my life to yours, for eternity.

I give you this ring as a sign of my devotion and love and with all my heart I promise to you, all that I am. With this ring I marry you and join my soul to yours.

❖

I give this ring in token and pledge of my constant faith and abiding love with all that I am and all that I will become, in the name of God.

❖

With this ring I promise to you my deepest love and devotion, for eternity.

❖

With this ring, I thee wed, as a symbol of love that is eternal.

❖

As this ring encircles your finger from this day forward, so will our souls forever be entwined.

❖

This ring I give you in token of my devotion and love, and with my soul I pledge to you all that I am. With this ring I marry you and join my life to yours.

❖

Non-spiritual Ring Exchanges

_____, I give you this ring as a symbol of my love. As it encircles your finger, may it remind you always that you are surrounded by my enduring love. Whenever you look at it, may it remind you of the vows we make today.

❖

This ring has no beginning and no ending, which symbolizes that the love between us will never cease. I place it on your finger as a visible sign of the vows, which have made us husband and wife.

❖

_____ I give you this ring as I give you myself. It is a circle without end. Such is my love for you.

❖

I give you this wedding ring, as a symbol of my unending love and devotion. May its presence on your hand serve always to remind you of my love.

❖

Just as this ring is without end, so my love for you is unending. Just as it is made of imperishable substance, my commitment to you will never fail. With this ring, I thee wed.

❖

I offer you this ring, shaped as a symbol of completeness, please wear this ring as a sign of our love and as a reminder of the promises we have made today.

❖

I give you this ring as a sign of my devotion and love and with all my heart I promise to you, all that I am. With this ring I marry you and join my life to yours.

❖

I give this ring in token and pledge of my constant faith and abiding love with all that I am and all that I will become.

❖

With this ring I promise to you my deepest love and devotion.

❖

With this ring, I wed you—for today, for tomorrow and for all the years to come. Please wear it as a sign of my love and a notice to all the world that you have chosen me to be your (husband/wife).

❖

This ring symbolizes the perfection of true love. As I place it on your finger, I give you all that I am and ever hope to be.

❖

May this ring remind you always of my love and the promises we've made here today.

❖

With this ring, I thee wed, as a symbol of love that has neither beginning nor end.

❖

I give you this ring; wear it with love and joy.

❖

As this ring encircles your finger from this day forward, so will my love forever encircle you.

❖

I give you this ring as a reminder that I love you every day of your life.

❖

This ring I give you in token of my devotion and love, and with my heart I pledge to you all that I am. With this ring I marry you and join my life to yours.

❖

I give you this ring to wear with love and joy. As this ring has no end, neither shall my love for you. I choose you to be my (wife/husband/partner) this day and every day.

❖

_____, this ring is a symbol, of my promise, to always be, your lover, companion, and friend.

❖

_____, in token and pledge, of the vow made between us, with this ring, I thee wed.

❖

I give you this ring, as a symbol of my love
And as a constant reminder
That I have chosen you, above all others
To be the one, to share my life.

Pronouncement of Marriage

Spiritual Pronouncements

_____ and _____ you have exchanged vows, promises and rings linking your destinies before God, family and friends, so by the will of God, I pronounce you husband and wife.

❖

_____ and _____ since you have each promised to the other your lifelong commitment, love and devotion, as a minister of the gospel, I pronounce you husband and wife; the grace of Christ attend you, the love of God surround you, the Holy Spirit keep you. Amen.

❖

_____ and _____ in God's presence and before family and friends, you have made your promises to be loving and faithful in your life together. Because of these promises, and by the giving and receiving of rings, I pronounce you husband and wife. What God has united let no one separate. In the name of the Father, the Son, and the Holy Spirit. Amen.

❖

_____ and _____, on behalf of all those present, and by the strength of your own love, I pronounce you married, and may the blessing of God be with you.

❖

Non-spiritual Pronouncements

_____ and _____ you have expressed your love to one another through the commitment and promises you have just made. It is with these in mind that I pronounce you husband and wife.

❖

_____ and _____ because you have promised each other your love, devotion and commitment, I declare you, husband and wife.

❖

_____ and _____ since you have exchanged vows and promised one another your never-ending love, commitment and loyalty, I pronounce you husband and wife.

❖

Now, because you have chosen one another, and vowed to love each other in marriage, it gives me great joy to pronounce you husband and wife.

❖

By the power vested in me by the state of _____, I now declare you, husband and wife.

❖

_____ and _____, on behalf of all those present, and by the strength of your own love, I pronounce you married.

❖

_____ and _____, because you have pledged your love and commitment to each other before these witnesses, I declare that you are husband and wife.

❖

Because of your choice to share a life, and the vows made here today, I pronounce you, husband and wife.

❖

The Kiss

You may kiss.

❖

You may kiss the bride.

❖

_____, you may kiss your bride.

❖

_____ and _____, you may now kiss to seal this union.

❖

You may kiss to seal this union.

❖

_____ and _____, you may seal your promises with a kiss.

❖

You may kiss to seal the bond of matrimony.

❖

You may kiss to seal your promises.

❖

You may kiss to seal this vow.

❖

Closing Blessings

Spiritual Blessings

Praised is love; blessed be this marriage. May the bride and groom rejoice together.

~ Joseph Campbell

❖

May this union between _____ and _____, provide the love and support for each of them to expand into their greatest purpose. As they now begin their journey together, we pray that God will continually guide their path both individually, and as a couple. Amen.

❖

The peace and serenity of the heavens be with you all. Amen

❖

May your marriage bring you all the exquisite excitements a marriage should bring, and may life grant you also patience, tolerance, and understanding. May you always need one another— not so much to fill your emptiness as to help you know your fullness. A mountain needs a valley to be complete; the valley does not make the mountain less, but more; and the valley is more a valley because it has a mountain towering over it. So let it be with you and you. May you need one another, but not out of weakness. May you want one another, but not out of lack. May you entice one another, but not compel one another. May you succeed in all-important ways with one another, and not fail in the little graces. May you look for things to praise, often say, "I love you!" and take no notice of small faults. If you have quarrels that push you apart, may both of you hope to have good sense enough to take the first step back. May you enter into the mystery, which is the awareness of one another's presence—no more physical than spiritual, warm and near when you are side-by-side, and warm and near when you are in separate rooms or even distant cities. May you have happiness, and may you find it making one another happy. May you have love, and may you find it loving one another!

~ *Blessing For A Marriage*, **James Dillet Freeman**

God, we ask that You please make _____ and _____'s relationship a great and sacred adventure. May their joining be a sacred space. May the two of them find rest here, a haven for their souls. Remove from them any temptation to judge one another or to direct one another. They surrender to you their conflicts and their burdens. They know you are their answer and their rock. Help them to not forget. Bring them together in heart and mind as well as body. Remove from them the temptation to criticize or be cruel. May they not be tempted by fantasies and projections. But guide them in the ways of holiness.

May this relationship be a burst of light. May it be a fount of love and wisdom for them, for their family, for their community, for the world. May this bond be a channel for your love and healing, a vehicle of Your grace and power. As lessons come and challenges grow, let them not be tempted to forsake each other. Let them always remember that in each other they have the most beautiful woman, the most beautiful man, The strongest one, The sacred one in whose arms they are repaired.

May they remain young in this relationship. Bring them what You desire for them, and show them how You would have them be. Thank You, dear God, you who are the cement between them. Thank You. Amen.

- Adapted from Illuminata, **Marianne Williamson**

Dear God, Please bring big life and big love, deep life and deep love. _____ and _____ wish to show up now with pure and noble hearts that they might engender the perfection in each other.

May they see each other's greatness and invoke each other's light. They surrender all the ways, both those they are aware of and those that remain unconscious, in which they block their love for each other. They surrender their defenses. They are ready to bring forth the holiest vibrations of love and healing between them. Where they are afraid to love, where they have built walls in front of their hearts, may they be healed and set free. Where they are needy or do not know how to behave or tend to control or to judge or to fix or be dishonest, please, dear God, show them another way.

They surrender theirselves to love. They surrender their love to You. May it serve Your purposes. May it receive Your blessing and carry Your power. May they never forsake each other. Thank You very much. Amen.

- Adapted from Illuminata, **Marianne Williamson**

God, we ask that you make ____ and ____'s relationship a wonderful and blessed adventure. May their joining together provide rest and protection for their souls. Guide their thoughts away from any temptation to judge or criticize one another and lead them to thoughts that support and build up one another. May their relationship be a source of love and wisdom for them, their family, their communities and the world. Help them to always remember that in each other they have the most beautiful person and carefully selected partner. Continuously show them what You desire for their marriage. Thank you, God. Amen.

❖

We ask God, that you bring expansive, deep, heart guided life and love to ____ and ____. May they continuously see each other's magnificence and surrender their defenses to bring forth the most sacred expression of their love for each other. We ask that you melt any walls that each one may have built over the years to protect their hearts. They now choose to surrender their hearts to Your greater purpose for their marriage. Thank you God. Amen.

❖

Dear Jesus, we ask in prayer that ____ and ____ be lifted up to you at this time, and that Your love and blessings take them by the hand, and guide them, as they walk in this new covenant with one another. May You provide the strength and encouragement to achieve any and all goals, overcome any and all trials, and persevere in love and commitment, as to Your will. It is in Your name, Jesus Christ, that we ask these blessings today. Amen.

~ Christopher Childers

Dear Jesus, We pray that you would bless this holy union and strengthen the bond of friendship that they have already established. We also pray that you would begin a lifetime of togetherness in the sanctity of what we call marriage, the joining together of two becoming one, in body, soul and spirit. And we pray that their decision today would be the same decision that they make every day from this point forward. That they would wake up each morning and say I choose you Jesus and also, I choose you _____ and I choose you _____. Thank you for this day and for these two. In Jesus name, Amen.

~ Pastor Delane Hollstein

May the road rise to meet you,
May the wind be always at your back.
May the sun shine warm upon your face,
The rains fall soft upon your fields.
And until we meet again,
May God hold you in the palm of his hand.
May God be with you and bless you;
May you see your children's children.
May you be poor in misfortune,
Rich in blessings,
May you know nothing but happiness
From this day forward.
May the road rise to meet you
May the wind be always at your back
May the warm rays of sun fall upon your home
And may the hand of a friend always be near.
May green be the grass you walk on,
May blue be the skies above you,
May pure be the joys that surround you,
May true be the hearts that love you.

~ Irish Blessing

Love has no other desire but to fulfill itself. But if you love and must needs have desires, let these be your desires: To melt and be like a running brook that sings its melody to the night. To know the pain of too much tenderness. To be wounded by your own understanding of love; and to bleed willingly and joyfully. To wake at dawn with a winged heart and give thanks for another day of loving; To rest at the noon hour and meditate love's ecstasy; To return home at eventide with gratitude; And then to sleep with a prayer for the beloved in your heart and a song of praise on your lips.

- "Love" from The Prophet, **Kahil Gibran**

Now you will feel no rain, for each of you will be shelter to the other. Now you will feel no cold, for each of you will be warmth to the other. Now you are two persons, but there is only one life before. Go now to your dwelling place to enter into the days of your life together. And may your days be good and long upon the earth.

Treat yourselves and each other with respect, and remind yourselves often of what brought you together. Give the highest priority to the tenderness, gentleness and kindness that your connection deserves. When frustration, difficulty and fear assail your relationship—as they threaten all relationships at one time or another—remember to focus on what is right between you, not only the part which seems wrong.

In this way, you can ride out the storms when clouds hide the face of the sun in your lives—remembering that even if you lose sight of it for a moment, the sun is still there. And if each of you takes responsibility for the quality of your life together, it will be marked by abundance and delight.

- APACHE MARRIAGE BLESSING

In the words of Shakespeare…

…A flock of blessings light upon thy back.

Or

…Look down you gods, and on this couple drop a blessed crown.

We know not what the future may bring into the lives of this couple, but we pray that together they may be equal to the needs of their tomorrows. I ask all of you who have heard the promises _____ and _____ have made to each other, to do everything in your power to support them, their commitment, and their marriage. If you agree to this, please respond by saying, "I will."
Guests: "I will!"

_____ and _____, you have declared your intention and vows before God, your families and friends. May the grace of this day carry forward in your marriage and may you continuously find delight in each other. May your love continue to grow and nourish you and may you always have the wisdom to cherish the precious love you share. May you each be guided by the loving spirit of God, nurturing yourselves and this marriage with acceptance, understanding, cooperation and love. May your life together be peaceful, healthy, and filled with blessings and joy.

_____ and _____, may you endlessly delight one another. May your love for each other continue to grow and deepen, providing a safe haven for your hearts. Go in peace. Live in joy. Thanks be to God.

_____ and _____, may your relationship be an example of the power of a deep and sustaining love. May you recognize God's presence every day. And may God bless your life together.

❖

_____ and _____, go in grace and love, seeing in each other the face of God smiling upon you and blessing you every day.

❖

My marriage prayer for you is this: That you will always remember the qualities that attracted you to each other when you first met and how you felt as your feelings of attraction turned into respect, admiration, and finally love. That you will work hard to turn your feelings of love into acts of love so that nothing and no one can divide you. That you will always have kind and loving hearts that are quick to ask for forgiveness when you are wrong and to forgive when your partner is wrong. That your love might grow to bear all things, believe all things, hope for all things, and endure all things. I pray you place your marriage in God's hands, and that your love increases and overflows, beyond anything you can yet imagine.

~ Carol Merolla

Lord, help us to remember when we first met and the strong love that grew between us. Help us to work that love into practical things so nothing can divide us. We ask for words both kind and loving, and for hearts always ready to ask forgiveness as well as to forgive. Dear Lord, we put our marriage into Your hands. Amen.

~ Author Unknown

To share in the splendor of the union of two souls is both an honor and a privilege in the company of love. May your union serve as a testimony to the undying love you share. May mountains move much easier with the burden split in two. We who've watched this relationship grow and bloom from the start are forever grateful to celebrate this new beginning with you. May you continue to grow together in peace and in love, and may your happiness be coupled with the love in your hearts forever.

~ Dawn M. Mueller

May the spirit that lives in and around all of us fill your hearts and bless your lives.

May you be blessed, every step of your path. May you endlessly delight one another. May you rest in the comfort of knowing that you have chosen through one another to serve the highest purposes of love. Depart in peace, recognizing that what you undertake together will bring you infinite joy.

~ adapted from Weddings from the Heart, **Daphne Rose Kingma**

Non-spiritual Wishes

Treat yourselves and each other with respect, and remind yourselves often of what brought you together. Give the highest priority to the tenderness, gentleness and kindness that your connection deserves.

When frustration, difficulty and fear assail your relationship— as they threaten all relationships at one time or another—remember to focus on what is right between you, not only the part which seems wrong. In this way, you can ride out the storms when clouds hide the face of the sun in your lives—remembering that even if you lose sight of it for a moment, the sun is still there. And if each of you takes responsibility for the quality of your life together, it will be marked by abundance and delight.

– APACHE MARRIAGE BLESSING (excerpt)

❖

May the significance of this moment and the vows and rings you have exchanged ever remain as a priceless memory in the heart of each of you and may you have perfect love and peace together.

❖

_____ and _____ if there is anything you remember of this marriage ceremony, may it be the love that brought you here today. It is only love which can make it a glorious union, and by love which your marriage shall endure. Today your separate lives with your individual memories, desires, and hopes merge into one. You are now taking into your care and keeping the happiness of the one person in the entire world whom you love above all others. You are adding to your life not only the affection of each other, but also the companionship and blessing of a deep trust as well. You are agreeing to share strength, responsibilities and to share love. May you be a blessing and comfort to each other, sharers of each other's dreams, consolers of each other's sorrows, helpers to each other in all of life's challenges. May you encourage each other in whatever you set out to achieve. May you trust each other, trust life and be unafraid. May your marriage bring you all the exquisite excitements a marriage should bring, and may life grant you patience, tolerance, and understanding.

❖

You share today the joy of a deep commitment and a sacred trust, and you have given each other the most precious gift of love. Treasure it, nurture it and encourage it with all the honesty you used in creating it. You are sharing something rare and beautiful. Always speak the truth and listen attentively so that you may understand each other's thoughts and intentions, inspire each other by sharing your accomplishments. Say "I love you" often to retain the warmth between you. Laugh a lot too, even when you are angry. Remember you are each other's best friend. Stand together and for each other always. May each day be a blessing and the fulfillment of your dreams.

~ Author Unknown

❖

In the words of Shakespeare…

…Fair thought and happy hours attend on you.

Or

…I wish you all the joy you can wish.

Or

…Love comforteth like sunshine after rain.

❖

May you look back on the past with as much pleasure as you look forward to the future.

~ Irish toast

❖

May their joys be as bright as the morning, and their sorrows but shadows that fade in the sunlight of love.

~ Armenian Blessing

❖

May their joys be as deep as the ocean and their misfortunes as light as the foam.

~ Armenian Blessing

❖

Ka mau ki aha. (May you never thirst again)

~ Traditional Hawaiian Wedding Toast

❖

May your hands be forever clasped in friendship and your hearts joined forever in love.

~ Traditional Blessing

❖

_____ and _____, there is an amazing life ahead of you. Live it fully. Love its changes and choices. Let life amaze you and bring you great joy.
May the love that you share give you strength
May the life that you share bring you joy
May the dreams that you share bring you hope
May the faith that you share bring you peace
And wherever you are in your journey through life,
May your hearts always find their way home. Amen.

*~ **Reverend J. Lynn James***

Presentations

Ladies and Gentlemen, may I (present/introduce) to you _____.

❖

Family and Friends, may I (present/introduce) to you _____.

❖

It is my (privilege/pleasure) to present to you _____.

❖

It is my honor to present to you for the first time _____.

❖

It is my pleasure to present to you the Newlyweds, _____ and _____ (last name).

❖

It is my pleasure to introduce to you, _____ and _____ (last name), [husband and wife].

❖

I introduce to you, _____ and _____ (last name), [husband and wife].

❖

Reading Selections

A Reading selection may be used in the place of any ceremony element, if it articulates what you want to convey for that element.

Spiritual Readings

We give of ourselves when we give gifts of the heart: love, kindness, joy, understanding, sympathy, tolerance, forgiveness.

We give of ourselves when we give gifts of the mind: ideas, dreams, purposes, ideals, principles, plans, inventions, projects, poetry.

We give of ourselves when we give gifts of the spirit: prayer, vision, beauty, aspiration, peace, faith.

We give of ourselves when we give the gift of words: encouragement, inspiration, guidance.

Emerson said it well: "Rings and jewels are not gifts, but apologies for gifts. The only true gift is a portion of thyself."

- *THE ART OF GIVING from "Art of Living",* **Wilfred A. Peterson**

❖

A soul mate is someone who has locks that fit our keys, and keys to fit our locks. When we feel safe enough to open the locks, our truest selves step out and we can be completely and honestly who we are; we can be loved for who we are and not for who we're pretending to be. Each unveils the best part of the other. No matter what else goes wrong around us, with that one person we're safe in our own paradise. Our soul mate is someone who shares our deepest longings, our sense of direction. When we're two balloons, and together our direction is up, chances are we've found the right person. Our soul mate is the one who makes life come to life.

– Excerpt from "The Bridge Across Forever", **Richard Bach**

If I could speak all the languages of earth and of angels, but didn't love others, I would only be a noisy gong or a clanging cymbal. If I had the gift of prophecy, and if I understood all of God's secret plans and possessed all knowledge, and if I had such faith that I could move mountains, but didn't love others, I would be nothing. If I gave everything I have to the poor and even sacrificed my body, I could boast about it; but if I didn't love others, I would have gained nothing.

Love is patient and kind. Love is not jealous or boastful or proud or rude. It does not demand its own way. It is not irritable, and it keeps no record of being wronged. It does not rejoice about injustice but rejoices whenever the truth wins out. Love never gives up, never loses faith, is always hopeful, and endures through every circumstance.

Prophecy and speaking in unknown languages and special knowledge will become useless. But love will last forever! Now our knowledge is partial and incomplete, and even the gift of prophecy reveals only part of the whole picture! But when full understanding comes, these partial things will become useless.

When I was a child, I spoke and thought and reasoned as a child. But when I grew up, I put away childish things. Now we see things imperfectly as in a cloudy mirror, but then we will see everything with perfect clarity. All that I know now is partial and incomplete, but then I will know everything completely, just as God now knows me completely.

Three things will last forever—faith, hope, and love—and the greatest of these is love.

~ I Corinthians 13:1-13 (also known as the "love chapter" of the Bible [New Living Translation])

Marriage is a commitment to life, the best that two people can find and bring out in each other. It offers opportunities for sharing and growth that no other relationship can equal. It is a physical and an emotional joining that is promised for a lifetime. Within the circle of its love, marriage encompasses all of life's most important relationships. A wife and a husband are each other's best friend, confidant, lover, teacher, listener, and critic. And there may come times when one partner is heartbroken or ailing, and the love of the other may resemble the tender caring of a parent for a child. Marriage deepens and enriches every facet of life. Happiness is fuller, memories are fresher, commitment is stronger, even anger is felt more strongly, and passes away more quickly. Marriage understands and forgives the mistakes life is unable to avoid. It encourages and nurtures new life, new experiences, and new ways of expressing a love that is deeper than life. When two people pledge their love and care for each other in marriage, they create a spirit unique unto themselves, which binds them closer than any spoken or written words. Marriage is a promise, a potential made in the hearts of two people who love each other and takes a lifetime to fulfill.

~ Marriage Joins Two People In The Circle Of Its Love, **Edmund O'Neill**

We, unaccustomed to courage
exiles from delight
live coiled in shells of loneliness
until love leaves its high holy temple
and comes into our sight
to liberate us into life.

Love arrives
and in its train come ecstasies
old memories of pleasure
ancient histories of pain.
Yet if we are bold,
love strikes away the chains of fear
from our souls.

We are weaned from our timidity
In the flush of love's light
we dare be brave
And suddenly we see
that love costs all we are
and will ever be.
Yet it is only love
which sets us free.

~ Touched by an Angel, **Maya Angelou**

Non-Spiritual Readings

Marriage is love walking hand in hand together. It's laughing with each other about silly little things, and learning to discuss big things with care and tenderness. In marriage, love is trusting each other when you're apart. It's getting over disappointments and hurts, knowing that these are present in all relationships. It's the realization that there is no one else in this world that you'd rather be with than the one you're married to. It's thinking of new things to do together; it's growing old together. Marriage is being in love for the rest of your life.

–Marriage Means Being In Love for the Rest of Your Life, **Chris Ardis**

True love is a sacred flame
That burns eternally,
And none can dim its special glow
Or change its destiny.
True love speaks in tender tones
And hears with gentle ear,
True love gives with open heart
And true love conquers fear.
True love makes no harsh demands
It neither rules nor binds,
And true love holds with gentle hands
The hearts that it entwines.

– True Love, **Author Unknown**

Sooner or later we begin to understand that love is more than verses on valentines, and romance in the movies. We begin to know that love is here and now, real and true, the most important thing in our lives. For love is the creator of our favorite memories, and the foundation of our fondest dreams. Love is a promise that is always kept, a fortune that can never be spent, a seed that can flourish in even the most unlikely of places. And this radiance that never fades, this mysterious and magical joy, is the greatest treasure of all—one known only by those who love.

– Sooner or Later, **Author Unknown**

The key to love is understanding ... The ability to comprehend not only the spoken word. But those unspoken gestures, the little things that say so much by themselves.

The key to love is forgiveness ... To accept each other's faults and pardon mistakes, without forgetting, but with remembering what you learn from them.

The key to love is sharing ... Facing your good fortunes as well as the bad, together; both conquering problems, forever searching for ways to intensify your happiness.

The key to love is giving ... Without thought of return, but with hope of just a simple smile, and by giving in but never giving up.

The key to love is respect ... Realizing that you are two separate people, with different ideas; that you don't belong to each other, that you belong with each other, and share a mutual bond.

The key to love is inside us all ... It takes time and patience to unlock all the ingredients that will take you to its threshold; it is the continual learning process that demands a lot of work ... but the rewards are more than worth the effort ... and that is the key to love.

- The Key to Love, **Anon**

If two are caring as they are sharing life's hopes and fears. If the music of laughter outweighs sadness and tears.

Marriage is togetherness.

If both derive pleasure from the mere presence of each other, yet when parted no jealousies restrict, worry or smother.

Marriage is freedom.

If achievements mean more when they benefit two and consideration is shown with each point of view.

Marriage is respect.

And if togetherness, freedom and respect are combined with a joy that words can never fully define, then...

Marriage is love.

- Marriage is Love, **Gloria Matthew**

It doesn't interest me what you do for a living. I want to know what you ache for and if you dare to dream of meeting your heart's longing.

It doesn't interest me how old you are. I want to know if you will risk looking like a fool for love, for your dream, for the adventure of being alive.

It doesn't interest me what planets are squaring your moon ... I want to know if you have touched the centre of your own sorrow, if you have been opened by life's betrayals or have become shriveled and closed from fear of further pain. I want to know if you can sit with pain, mine or your own without moving to hide it, or fade it, or fix it.

I want to know if you can be with joy, mine or your own, if you can dance with wildness and let the ecstasy fill you to the tips of your fingers and toes without cautioning us to, be careful, be realistic, remember the limitations of being human.

It doesn't interest me if the story you are telling me is true. I want to know if you can disappoint another to be true to yourself. If you can bear the accusation of betrayal and not betray your own soul. If you can be faithless and therefore trustworthy.

I want to know if you can see Beauty even when it is not pretty every day. And if you can source your own life from its presence. I want to know if you can live with failure, yours and mine and still stand at the edge of the lake and shout to the silver of the full moon, "Yes."

It doesn't interest me to know where you live or how much money you have. I want to know if you can get up after the night of grief and despair weary and bruised to the bone and do what needs to be done to feed the children.

It doesn't interest me who you know or how you came to be here. I want to know if you will stand in the centre of the fire with me and not shrink back.

It doesn't interest me where or what or with whom you have

studied. I want to know what sustains you from the inside when all else falls away.

I want to know if you can be alone with yourself and if you truly like the company you keep in the empty moments.

- The Invitation, **Oriah**

❖

Love is . . . Being happy for the other person when they are happy, Being sad for the person when they are sad, Being together in good times, And being together in bad times.

Love is the source of Strength.

Love is . . . Being honest with yourself at all times, Being honest with the other person at all times, Telling, listening, respecting the truth, And never pretending.

Love is the source of Reality.

Love is . . . An understanding so complete that you feel as if you are a part of the other person, Accepting the other person just the way they are, And not trying to change them to be something else.

Love is the source of Unity.

Love is . . . The freedom to pursue your own desires while sharing your experiences with the other person, The growth of one individual alongside of and together with the growth of another individual.

Love is the source of Success.

Love is . . . The excitement of planning things together, the excitement of doing things together.

Love is the source of the Future.

Love is . . . The fury of the storm, The calm in the rainbow.

Love is the source of Passion.

Love is . . . Giving and taking in a daily situation, being patient with each other's needs and desires.

Love is the source of Sharing.

Love is . . . Knowing that the other person will always be with you regardless of what happens, Missing the other person when they are away but remaining near in heart at all times.

Love is the source of Security.
Love is . . . the source of Life!

- *Love Is,* **Susan Polis Schutz**

I can not promise you that I will not change
I can not promise you that I will not have many different moods
I cannot promise you that I will not hurt your feelings sometimes
I can not promise you that I will not be erratic
I can not promise you that I will always be strong
I can not promise you that my faults will not show
But, I do promise you that I will always be supportive of you
I do promise you that I will share all my thoughts and feelings with you
I do promise you that I will give you freedom to be yourself
I do promise you that I will understand everything that you do
I do promise you that I will be completely honest with you
I do promise you that I will laugh and cry with you
I do promise you that I will help you achieve all your goals
But, most of all I do promise you that I love you

- *I Love You,* **Susan Polis Schutz**

To love is to enter a whole new world of togetherness, a world of sharing all that is dearest and deepest within your hearts. To love is to remember and keep alive forever all those unique qualities that drew you to one another in the beginning and that wonderful feeling of oneness when your eyes first met. To love is to constantly search for new ways to bring each other happiness, to make the most of every moment you share together, and marvel at how your feelings for one another keep rising to new dimensions.

To love is to create an oasis of tranquility for one another and a quiet place, apart from others, where you need not pretend ...

where you can be yourselves ... And know within your hearts, you will be accepted by one another. To love is to greet each day with anticipation ... Always eager for another opportunity to share new adventures, and gather up new memories together!

To love is to follow the rainbow through the rain, to be able to laugh at yourselves and be willing to say, "I was wrong, I'm sorry," to forgive, and more importantly, to forget, and to always believe and trust in one another. To love is to watch with wonder all the miracles of creation, to find beauty in all the simple things of life, and to find, within yourselves, a deeper appreciation and a new awareness of how wonderful it is to be alive, to be happy, to be together.

To love is coming together from the pathways of your past and then moving forward, hand in hand, along the uncharted roads of your future, ready to risk, to dream, and to dare. Always believing that all things are possible with faith and love.

– To Love, **Author Unknown**

Love, I love you not only for what you are, but for what I am when I am with you. I love you, not only for what you have made of yourself, but for what you are making of me. I love you for the part of me that you bring out.

I love you for reaching out and touching my heart, and passing over all the foolish, weak things that you can't help simply seeing there. And for drawing out into the light all the beautiful belongings, that no one else had looked quite far enough to find.

Love is entrusting our faults to one another. Love is belonging in each other's thoughts with care as well as feeling. Love is beautiful. You are enhanced by my love.

I am enhanced by you, Love. I love because of you, and you are the reason for all of my tomorrows. Your love makes my life complete.

Love – adapted from poem by **Roy Croft**

I promise to give you the best of myself and to ask of you no more than you can give.

I promise to respect you as your own person and to realize that your interests, desires and needs are no less important than my own.

I promise to share with you my time and my attention and to bring joy, strength and imagination to our relationship.

I promise to keep myself open to you, to let you see through the window of my world into my innermost fears and feelings, secrets and dreams.

I promise to grow along with you, to be willing to face changes in order to keep our relationship alive and exciting.

I promise to love you in good times and in bad, with all I have to give and all I feel inside, in the only way I know how. Completely and forever.

- I Promise, Dorothy Colgan

Doubt thou the stars are fire;
Doubt that the sun doth move;
Doubt truth to be a liar;
But never doubt I love.

- From Hamlet, William Shakespeare

Let me not to the marriage of true minds admit impediments.
Love is not love which alters when it alteration finds,
or bends with the remover to remove:
Oh, no! It is an ever-fixed mark.
That looks on tempests and is never shaken;
it is the star to every wandering bark,
whose worth's unknown, although his height be taken.
Love's not Time's fool, though rosy lips and cheeks
within his bending sickle's compass come;

love alters not with his brief hours and weeks,
but bears it out even to the edge of doom.
If this be error and upon me proved,
I never writ, nor no man ever loved.

~ Sonnet 116, **William Shakespeare**

My bounty is as boundless as the sea,
My love as deep:
The more I give to thee,
The more I have,
For both are infinite.

~ From Romeo and Juliet, **William Shakespeare**

The way to happiness: Keep your heart free from hate, your mind from worry. Live simply. Expect little. Give much.

~ Traditional saying

I am not sure that the Earth is round, nor that the sky is really blue. The tale of why the apples fall, may or may not be true. I do not know what makes the tides, nor what tomorrow's world may do. But I have certainty enough, For I am sure of you.

*~ **Amelia Josephine Burr***

She walks in Beauty, like the night
Of cloudless climes and starry skies;
And all that's best of dark and bright
Meet in her aspect and her eyes:
Thus mellowed to that tender light
Which Heaven to gaudy day denies.

*~ **Lord Byron***

You will find as you look back upon your life that the moments when you have truly lived are the moments when you have done things in the spirit of love.

*~ **Henry Drummond***

The minute I heard my first love story I started looking for you, not knowing how blind that was. Lovers don't finally meet somewhere. They're in each other all along.

~ The Ruins of the Heart (Version 1), **Rumi**

The moment I heard my first love story I began seeking you, not realizing the search was useless. Lovers don't meet somewhere along the way. They're in one another's souls from the beginning.

~ The Ruins of the Heart (Version 2), **Rumi**

Happiness in a marriage is not something that just happens; a good marriage must be created. And it is created in the following ways:

It is never being too old to hold hands.

It is remembering to say "I love you" at least once a day.

It is at no time taking the other for granted.

It is having a mutual sense of values and common objectives.

It is standing together facing life.

It is forming a circle of love that gathers in the whole family.

It is doing things for each other not in the attitude of duty or sacrifice, but in the spirit of joy.

It is speaking words of appreciation and demonstrating gratitude.

It is not looking for perfection in each other.

It is cultivating flexibility, patience, understanding, and a sense of humor.

It is having the capacity to forgive and forget.

It is giving each other an atmosphere in which each can grow.

It is finding room for the things of the spirit.

It is a common search for the good and the beautiful.

It is establishing a relationship in which independence is equal, dependence is mutual, and obligation is reciprocal. It is not only marrying the right partner, it is being the right partner.

~Rev. Bill Swetmon

1. Never both be angry at the same time.
2. Never yell at each other unless the house is on fire.
3. If one of you has to win an argument, let it be your mate.
4. If you must criticize, do it lovingly.
5. Never bring up mistakes of the past.
6. Neglect the whole world rather than each other.
7. Never go to sleep with an argument unsettled.
8. At least once every day say a kind or complimentary word to your life partner.
9. When you have done something wrong, admit it and ask for forgiveness.
10. Remember it takes two to make a quarrel.

- "Ten Rules for a Happy Marriage", from a couple who reached 50 years of marriage, **Dear Abby**

Love alone is capable of uniting living beings in such a way as to complete and fulfill them, for it alone takes them and joins them by what is deepest in themselves.

- From The Phenomenon of Man, **Pierre Teilhard de Chardin**

When one has once fully entered the realm of love, the world—no matter how imperfect—becomes rich and beautiful, for it consists solely of opportunities for love.

~Soren Kierkegaard

Thou art the star that guides me along life's changing sea; And whate'er fate betides me, this heart still turns to thee.

~ George Morris

In a time when nothing is more certain than change, the commitment of two people to one another has become difficult and rare. Yet, by its scarcity, the beauty and value of this exchange have only been enhanced.

From "The Vow", **Robert Sexton**

You are my husband
My feet shall run because of you
My feet dance because of you
My heart shall beat because of you
My eyes see because of you
My mind thinks because of you
And I shall love because of you.

~ ESKIMO LOVE SONG

No man ever forgot the visitation of that power to his heart and brain, which created all things anew; which was the dawn in him of music, poetry and art; which made the face of nature radiant with purple light, the morning and the night varied enchantments; … when he became all eye when one was present, and all memory when one was gone.

~ Ralph Waldo Emerson

And now here is my secret, a very simple secret: it is only with the heart that one can see rightly; what is essential is invisible to the eye …

~ Antoine de Saint-Exupéry

Married love is love woven into a pattern of living. It has in it the elements of understanding and of the passionate kindness of husband and wife towards each other. It is rich in the many-sided joys of life because each is more concerned with giving joy than with grasping it for himself. And joys are most truly experienced when they are most fully shared.

~ Leland Foster Wood

Do not think that love, in order to be genuine, has to be extraordinary. What we need is to love without getting tired.

~ Mother Teresa

Marriage has too often been portrayed as two people frozen together side by side, as immobile as marble statues. More accurately, it is the intricate and graceful cooperation of two dancers who through long practice have learned to match each other's movements and moods in response to the music.

~ David R. Mace

I have no desire to move mountains, construct monuments, or leave behind in my wake material evidence of my existence. But in the final recollection, if the essence of my being has caused a smile to have appeared upon your face or a touch of joy within your heart, then in living, I have made my mark.

~ Thomas L. Odem Jr.

Don't walk in front of me, I may not follow.
Don't walk behind me, I may not lead.
Just walk beside me and be my friend.

~ Albert Camus

❖

Readings ~ from Movies

A Beautiful Mind

"It's only in the mysterious equations of love that any logical reasons can be found. I am only here tonight because of you. You are all I am. You are all my reasons."

The Bridges of Madison County

- "It seems right now that all I've ever done in my life is making my way here to you."

- "This kind of certainty comes but once in a lifetime."

Captain Corelli's Mandolin

"When you fall in love, it is a temporary madness. It erupts like an earthquake, and then it subsides. And when it subsides, you have to make a decision. You have to work out whether your roots have become so entwined together that it is inconceivable that you should ever part. Because this is what love is. Love is not breathlessness, it is not excitement, it is not the promulgation of promises of eternal passion. That is just being in love, which any of us can convince ourselves we are. Love itself is what is left over when being in love has burned away."

City of Angels

- "I would rather have had one breath of her hair, one kiss from her mouth, one touch of her hand, than eternity without it."

- "When they ask me what I liked best, I'll say it was you."

Crouching Tiger, Hidden Dragon

- "A faithful heart makes wishes come true."

- "I would rather be a ghost drifting by your side as a condemned soul than enter heaven without you. Because of your love, I will never be a lonely spirit."

- "I want to tell you with my last breath that I have always loved you."

Don Juan DeMarco

"There are only four questions of value in life. What is sacred? Of what is the spirit made of? What is worth living for? What is worth dying for? The answer to each is the same. Only love."

Forces of Nature

"I always thought that there was this one perfect person for everybody in the world and when you found that person, the rest of the world just kind of magically faded away and the two of you would just be inside this kind of protective bubble. But there is no bubble. Or if there is, we have to make it. I just think life is more than a series of moments … we can make choices and we can choose to protect the people we love and that's what makes us who we are and those are the real miracles. I fell in love with you the moment I saw you … when I'm on my death bed, I'm gonna know that I married the only woman I ever really loved."

The Notebook

- "The best love is the kind that awakens the soul and makes us reach for more, that plants a fire in our hearts and brings peace to our minds and that's what you've given me."

- "I am nothing special; just a common man with common thoughts, and I've led a common life. There are no monuments dedicated to me, and my name will soon be forgotten. But in one respect I have succeeded as gloriously as anyone who's ever lived: I've loved another with all my heart and soul and to me, this has always been enough."

The Phantom of the Opera

"Say you'll share with me one love, one lifetime. Lead me, save me from my solitude. Say you want me with you, here beside you. Anywhere you go, let me go, too. Love me, that's all I ask of you."

Runaway Bride

"Look. I guarantee there'll be tough times. I guarantee that at some point, one or both of us is gonna want to get out of this thing. But, I also guarantee that if I don't ask you to be mine, I'll regret it for the rest of my life, because I know, in my heart, you're the only one for me."

Shakespeare In Love

- "I will have poetry in my life. And adventure. And love. Love above all. No ... not the artful postures of love, not playful and poetical games of love for the amusement of an evening, but love that ... overthrows life. Unbiddable, ungovernable, like a riot in the heart, and nothing to be done, come ruin or rapture."

- "Love denied blights the soul we owe to God."

- "If I could write the beauty of her eyes, I was born to look into them and know myself."

Shall We Dance

"We need a witness to our lives. There's a billion people on the planet ... I mean, what does any one life mean? But in a marriage, you're promising to care about everything. The good things, the bad things, the terrible things, the mundane things ... all of it, all the time, every day. You're saying 'Your life will not go unnoticed because I will notice it. Your life will not go unwitnessed because I will be your witness'."

Sideways

Miles (trying to explain to Maya why he is so interested in Pinot Noir wine): "It's a hard grape to grow. As you know. Right? It's, uh, it's thin-skinned, temperamental, ripens early.

It's, you know, it's not a survivor like cabernet, which can just grow anywhere and thrive even when it's neglected. No, pinot needs constant care and attention. You know? And, in fact, it can only grow in these really specific, little tucked-away corners of the world. And only the most patient and nurturing of growers can do it, really. Only somebody who really takes the time to understand pinot's potential can then coax it into its fullest expression."

Sleepless In Seattle

"Well, it was a million tiny little things that, when you add them all up, they meant that we were supposed to be together ... and I knew it. I knew it the very first time I touched her. It was like coming home ... only to no home I'd ever known. I was just taking her hand to help her out of a car and I knew. It was like ... magic."

Somewhere in Time

"If I could measure the beauty of her eyes, I was born to look in them and know myself."

Star Wars: Episode II - Attack of the Clones

Anakin to Padme: "From the moment I met you, all those years ago, not a day has gone by when I haven't thought of you. And now that I'm with you again ... I'm in agony. The closer I get to you, the worse it gets. The thought of not being with you—I can't breath. I'm haunted by the kiss that you should never have given me. My heart is beating ... hoping that kiss will not become a scar. You are in my very soul, tormenting me ... what can I do?—I will do anything you ask."

The Two Towers - *by J.R.R. Tolkien*
(Treebeard's Song of the Entwives)

ENT: When Spring unfolds the beechen leaf, and sap is in the bough; When light is on the wild-wood stream, and wind is on the brow; When stride is long, and breath is deep, and keen the mountain-air, Come back to me! Come back to me, and say my land is fair!

ENTWIFE: When Spring is come to garth and field, and corn is in the blade; When blossom like a shining snow is on the orchard laid; When shower and Sun upon the Earth with fragrance fill the air, I'll linger here, and will not come, because my land is fair.

ENT: When Summer lies upon the world, and in a noon of gold beneath the roof of sleeping leaves the dreams of trees unfold; When woodland halls are green and cool, and wind is in the West, Come back to me! Come back to me, and say my land is best!

ENTWIFE: When Summer warms the hanging fruit and burns the berry brown; When straw is gold, and ear is white, and harvest comes to town; When honey spills, and apple swells, though wind be in the West, I'll linger here beneath the Sun, because my land is best!

ENT: When Winter comes, the winter wild that hill and wood shall slay; When trees shall fall and starless night devour the sunless day; When wind is in the deadly East, then in the bitter rain I'll look for thee, and call to thee; I'll come to thee again!

ENTWIFE: When Winter comes, and singing ends; when darkness falls at last; When broken is the barren bough, and light and labour past; I'll look for thee, and wait for thee, until we meet again: Together we will take the road beneath the bitter rain!

BOTH: Together we will take the road that leads into the West, And far away will find a land where both our hearts may rest.

A Walk to Remember

- "Jamie saved my life. She taught me everything. About life, hope and the long journey ahead. I'll always miss her. But our love is like the wind. I can't see it, but I can feel it."

- "Love is always patient and kind. It is never jealous. Love is never boastful or conceited. It is never rude or selfish. It does not take pleasure in other people's sins, but delights in the truth. It is always ready to excuse, to trust, to hope, and to endure whatever comes."

The Wedding Singer ~ *Adam Sandler*

"I think we all know that when you fall in love, the emptiness kind of drifts away ... because you find something to live for. Each other. And the way I see you two looking into each other's eyes all day long, I can tell that you're going to live for each other for the rest of your lives."

The Wedding Date

- "... I think I'd miss you even if we'd never met."

- "The hardest part of love isn't loving someone, but having the courage to let them love you back."

When Harry Met Sally

- "I love that you get cold when it's seventy degrees out. I love that it takes you an hour and a half to order a sandwich. I love that you get a little crinkle above your nose when you're looking at me like I'm nuts. I love that after I spend a day with you I can still smell your perfume on my clothes, and I love that you are the last person I want to talk to before I go to sleep at night."

- "When you realize you want to spend the rest of your life with somebody, you want the rest of your life to start as soon as possible."

From TV....

If I had this day to live over, I wouldn't change one blessed thing. Not one step that got me here with you, right now. I want to be here. I belong here. I love you more than anything. And what's more ... I don't want to live without you. You are an answer to a very big question: Where's the rest of my heart? ... You're in my blood. You're in a place in me so deep no one else is ever gonna be able to get there again.

- TV drama, **All My Children***, 1989*

I want to wake up with you every morning and fall asleep next to you every night. I want to laugh and dream and fight and make up. I want to make babies, mistakes, music, and magic to really live. All with you.

- TV drama, **One Life to Live***, 1993*

Marriage means work, attention, care, unconditional love, acceptance of each other's imperfections, and adjustments. But if you've chosen the right partner, then nothing in your life can be more rewarding.

- TV drama, **General Hospital***, 1996*

Readings ~ from Song Lyrics

Let me be your freedom,
let daylight dry your tears.
I'm here with you, beside you,
to guard you and to guide you …

Say you love me every waking moment,
turn my head with talk of summertime …
Say you need me with you now and always …
Promise me that all you say is true,
that's all I ask of you …

Let me be your shelter,
let me be your light.

Then say you'll share with me one love, one lifetime …
let me lead you from your solitude …
Say you need me with you here, beside you …
anywhere you go, let me go too—
say the word and I will follow you …

Share each day with me,
each night,
each morning …
Say you love me …
You know I do …
Love me—that's all I ask of you …

- All I Ask of You (Excerpt), **Phantom of the Opera**

At last
my love has come along
my lonely days over
and life is like a song

I found a dream
that I could speak to
a dream that I could call my own
I found a thrill
to press my cheek to
a thrill that I have never known

You smile
and then the spell was cast
and here we are in heaven
for you are mine at last

~ At Last (Excerpt), **Ella Fitzgerald**

I don't want another pretty face
I don't want just anyone to hold
I don't want my love to go to waste
I want you and your beautiful soul
You're the one I wanna chase
You're the one I wanna hold
I won't let another minute go to waste
I want you and your beautiful soul

I know that you are something special
To you I'd be always faithful
I want to be what you always needed
Then I hope you'll see the heart in me
I want you and your beautiful soul

~ Beautiful Soul (Excerpt), **Jesse McCartney**

Oh my life
Is changing everyday
In every possible way
And Oh my dreams
It's never quite as it seems
Never quite as it seems

I know I've felt like this before
But now I'm feeling it even more
Because it came from you

And then I open up and see
The person falling here is me
A different way to be
I want more (impossible to ignore)
And they'll come true (impossible not to do)

And now I tell you openly
You have my heart so don't hurt me
You're what I couldn't find

A totally amazing mind
So understanding and so kind
You're everything to me

- Dreams (Excerpt), **Cranberries**

Grow old along with me, the best is yet to be
When our time has come, we will be as one
God bless our love

Grow old along with me, two branches of one tree
Face the setting sun, when the day is done
God bless our love

Spending our lives together, man and wife together
World without end,
Grow old along with me, whatever fate decrees
We will see it through, for our love is true
God bless our love

- Grow Old with Me (Excerpt), **John Lennon**

I wanna make you smile whenever you're sad
Carry you around when your arthritis is bad
All I wanna do is grow old with you

I'll get your medicine when your tummy aches
Build you a fire if the furnace breaks
Oh it could be so nice, growing old with you

I'll miss you
Kiss you
Give you my coat when you are cold

Need you
Feed you
Even let ya hold the remote control

So let me do the dishes in our kitchen sink
Put you to bed if you've had too much to drink
I could be the man who grows old with you
I wanna grow old with you

~ *Grow Old with You (Excerpt)*, **Adam Sandler**

Maybe it's intuition
But some things you just don't question
Like in your eyes
I see my future in an instant
And there it goes
I think I've found my best friend
I know that it might sound more than a little crazy
But I believe
I knew I loved you before I met you
I think I dreamed you into life
I knew I loved you before I met you
I have been waiting all my life

There's just no rhyme or reason
Only this sense of completion
And in your eyes
I see the missing pieces
I'm searching for
I think I've found my way home

~ I knew I Loved You (Excerpt), **Savage Garden**

My love must be a kind of blind love
I can't see anyone but you
And dear, I wonder if you find love
An optical illusion, too?

Are the stars out tonight?
I don't know if it's cloudy or bright
'Cause I only have eyes for you, dear
The moon may be high
But I can't see a thing in the sky
'Cause I only have eyes for you.

I don't know if we're in a garden
Or on a crowded avenue
You are here, so am I
Maybe millions of people go by
But they all disappear from view
And I only have eyes for you

~ I Only Have Eyes for You (Excerpt), **Al Dubin**

If there were no words
No way to speak
I would still hear you

If there were no tears
No way to feel inside
I'd still feel for you

And even if the sun refused to shine
Even if romance ran out of rhyme
You would still have my heart
Until the end of time
You're all I need
My love, my Valentine

All of my life
I have been waiting for
All you give to me
You've opened my eyes
And shown me how to love unselfishly

I've dreamed of this a thousand times before
In my dreams I couldn't love you more
I will give you my heart
Until the end of time
You're all I need
My love, my Valentine

- Valentine (Excerpt), **Jim Brickman**

It's hard for me to say the things
I want to say sometimes
There's no one here but you and me
And that broken old street light
Lock the doors
We'll leave the world outside
All I've got to give to you
Are these five words when I

Thank you for loving me
For being my eyes
When I couldn't see
For parting my lips
When I couldn't breathe
Thank you for loving me

I never knew I had a dream
Until that dream was you
When I look into your eyes
The sky's a different blue
Cross my heart
I wear no disguise
If I tried, you'd make believe
That you believed my lies
Thank you for loving me

~ *Thank You for Loving Me (Excerpt),* **Jon Bon Jovi**

I'll be your dream,
I'll be your wish
I'll be your fantasy.
I'll be your hope,
I'll be your love
be everything that you need.
I love you more with every breath
truly madly deeply do …
I will be strong I will be faithful
cause I'm counting on
A new beginning.
A reason for living.
A deeper meaning.

I want to stand with you on a mountain.

I want to bathe with you in the sea.
I want to lay like this forever.
Until the sky falls down on me ...

And when the stars are shining
brightly in the velvet sky,
I'll make a wish send it to heaven
then make you want to cry ...
the tears of joy for all the pleasure
and the certainty
that we're surrounded by the comfort
and protection of ...
the highest power.

I'll love you more with every breath
truly madly deeply do ...

~ Truly Madly Deeply (Excerpt), **Savage Garden**

I see trees of green, red roses too
I see them bloom for me and you
And I think to myself what a wonderful world.

I see skies of blue and clouds of white
The bright blessed day, the dark sacred night
And I think to myself what a wonderful world.

The colors of the rainbow so pretty in the sky
Are also on the faces of people going by
I see friends shaking hands saying how do you do
They're really saying I love you.

I hear babies crying, I watch them grow
They'll learn much more than I'll never know
And I think to myself what a wonderful world

~ What a Wonderful World (Excerpt), **Louis Armstrong**

There are places I remember
All my life, though some have changed
Some forever not for better
Some have gone and some remain
All these places had their moments
With lovers and friends
I still can recall
Some are dead and some are living
In my life I've loved them all

But of all these friends and lovers
there is no one compares with you
And these memories lose their meaning
When I think of love as something new
Though I know I'll never lose affection
For people and things that went before
I know I'll often stop and think about them
In my life I love you more

- In My Life (Excerpt), **Beatles**

Tomorrow morning if you wake up and the sun does not appear
I will be here
If in the dark, we lose sight of love
Hold my hand, and have no fear
'Cause I will be here

I will be here
When you feel like being quiet
When you need to speak your mind
I will listen
And I will be here
When the laughter turns to cryin'
Through the winning, losing and trying
We'll be together

I will be here
Tomorrow morning, if you wake up
And the future is unclear
I will be here
Just as sure as seasons were made for change
Our lifetimes were made for these years
So I will be here

I will be here
And you can cry on my shoulder
When the mirror tells us we're older
I will hold you
And I will be here
To watch you grow in beauty
And tell you all the things you are to me
I will be here

I will be true to the promise I have made
To you and to the One who gave you to me

Tomorrow morning, if you wake up
And the sun does not appear
I will be here
Oh, I will be here

~ I Will Be Here (Excerpt), **Steven Curtis Chapman**

I'll take care of you
Don't be sad, don't be blue
I'll never break your heart in two
I'll take care of you

I'll take care of you
I'll kiss your tears away

I'll end your lonely days
All that I'm trying to say
Is I'll take care of you

I want you to know that I love you so
I'm proud to tell the world you're mine
I said it before, I'll say it once more
You'll be in my heart 'til the end of time

I'll take care of you
Don't be sad, don't be blue
Just count on me your whole life through
'Cause I'll take care of you

~ *I'll Take Care of You (Excerpt)*, **Archie Jordan and Glenn Sutton**

Readings ~ from Children's Stories

"What is REAL?" asked the Rabbit one day, when they were lying side by side near the nursery fender, before Nana came to tidy the room. "Does it mean having things that buzz inside you and a stick-out handle?"

"Real isn't how you are made," said the Skin Horse. "It's a thing that happens to you. When a child loves you for a long, long time, not just to play with, but Really loves you, then you become Real."

"Does it hurt?" asked the Rabbit.

"Sometimes," said the Skin Horse, for he was always truthful. "When you are Real you don't mind being hurt."

"Does it happen all at once, like being wound up," he asked, "or bit by bit?"

"It doesn't happen all at once," said the Skin Horse. "You become. It takes a long time. That's why it doesn't happen often to people who break easily, or have sharp edges, or who have to be carefully kept. Generally, by the time you are Real, most of your hair has been loved off, and your eyes drop out and you get all loose in the joints and very shabby. But these things don't matter at all, because once you are Real you can't be ugly, except to people who don't understand."

- Excerpt from The Velveteen Rabbit, By **Margery Williams**

Congratulations
Today is your day
You're off to Great Places
You're off and away!
You have brains in your head.
You have feet in your shoes
You can steer yourself any direction you choose.
You're now on your own. And you know what you know.
And YOU are the couple who'll decide where to go.

You'll look up and down streets. Look 'em over with care.
About some you will say, "I don't choose to go there."
With your head full of brains and your shoes full of feet,
you're too smart to go down any not-so-good street.

OH! THE PLACES YOU'LL GO!

You'll be on your way up!
You'll be seeing great sights!
You'll join the high fliers who soar to high heights

On and on you will hike and I know you'll hike far
and face up to your problems whatever they are.

You'll get mixed up, of course, as you already know.

You'll get mixed up with many strange birds as you go.
So be sure when you step. Step with care and great tact
and remember that Life's a Great Balancing Act.
Just never forget to be dexterous and deft.
And never mix up your right foot with your left.

And will you succeed?
Yes! You will, indeed!
(98 and 3/4 percent guaranteed.)

KIDS, YOU'LL MOVE MOUNTAINS!

So ...
you're off to Great Places!
Today IS your day!
Your mountain is waiting.
So ... get on your way!

- Adapted from "Oh, the Places You'll Go!", **Dr. Seuss**

I'll love you forever,
I'll like you for always,
As long as I'm living
My [love] you'll be.

- Adapted from Love You Forever, **Robert Munsch**

If you become a fish in a trout stream, I will become a fisherman and I will fish for you.

If you become a rock on the mountain high above me, I will be a mountain climber, and I will climb to where you are.

If you become a crocus in a hidden garden, I will be a garden. And I will find you.

If you become a bird and fly away from me, I will be a tree that you come home to.

If you go flying on a flying trapeze, I will be a tightrope walker, and I will walk across the air to you.

Wherever you go, whatever you become, I will always be here to catch you in my arms and hug you.

– Adapted from Runaway Bunny, **Margaret Wise Brown**

❖

Readings ~ Humor

Marriage resembles a pair of shears, so joined that they cannot be separated; often moving in opposite directions, yet always punishing anyone who comes between them.

~ Sydney Smith

❖

Marriage is a matter of give and take, but so far I haven't been able to find anybody who'll take what I have to give.

~ Cass Daley

❖

On the way to the airport after the wedding, the bride asked her husband, a bachelor for forty years, if he had their plane tickets. He confidently reached into his pocket … and then saw that out of habit, he had bought just one ticket. "Incredible! Just one ticket. You know, dear, I've been married only an hour and already I've forgotten about myself."

~Anonymous

Harpo, she's a lovely person. She deserves a good husband. Marry her before she finds one.

~ **Oscar Levant** (spoken to Harpo Marx upon meeting Harpo's fiancé)

To keep your marriage brimming, with love in the wedding cup, whenever you're wrong, admit it; whenever you're right, shut up.

~ **Ogden Nash**

Laugh and the world laughs with you. Snore and you sleep alone.

~ **Anthony Burgess**

Love is being stupid together.

~ **Paul Valéry**

Marriage is a continuous process of getting used to things you hadn't expected.

~ **Anonymous**

Anyone can be passionate, but it takes real lovers to be silly.

~ **Rose Franken**

Quotes ~ Spiritual

Hereafter in a better world than this, I shall desire more love and knowledge of you.

~ **William Shakespeare**

A heaven on earth I have won by wooing thee.

~ William Shakespeare

❖

I have found the one whom my soul loves.

~ Song of Solomon 3:4

❖

Love makes your soul crawl out from its hiding place.

~ Zora Neale Hurston

❖

The crossing of the threshold is the first step into the sacred zone of the Universal source.

~ Joseph Campbell

❖

Two human loves make one divine.

~ Elizabeth Barrett Browning

❖

Quotes ~ Non-spiritual

The Nyinba (Tibetans of northwest Nepal) have no word for "Love." They call it, "Beautiful from the heart."

❖

Love is the greatest refreshment in life.

~ Pablo Picasso

❖

To love is to admire with the heart.

~ Theophile Gautier

❖

With one glance, I loved you with a thousand hearts.

~ Mihri Hatun

❖

To love someone is to see a miracle invisible to others.

~ François Mauriac

❖

When the satisfaction or security of another person becomes as significant to one as one's own satisfaction or security, then the state of love exists.

~Harry Stack Sullivan

❖

Success in marriage is much more than finding the right person; it is a matter of being the right person.

~ B. R. Brickner

❖

I am, in every thought of my heart, yours.

~ Woodrow Wilson

❖

The best and most beautiful things in the world cannot be seen or even touched. They must be felt with the heart.

~ Helen Keller

❖

Never above you.
Never below you.
Always beside you.

~ Walter Winchell

❖

Love is, above all, the gift of oneself.

~ Jean Anouilh

❖

Love is the wine of existence.

~Henry Ward Beecher

❖

Love is always bestowed as a gift –freely, willingly and without expectation.

~ Leo Buscaglia

❖

A friend knows the song in my heart and sings it to me when my memory fails.

~ Donna Roberts

❖

Love does not consist of gazing at each other but in looking together in the same direction.

~ Antoine de Saint-Exupéry

❖

We attract hearts by the qualities we display: we retain them by the qualities we possess.

~ Jean Suard

❖

Let us always meet each other with a smile, for a smile is the beginning of love.

~ Mother Teresa

❖

In this life we cannot do great things. We can only do small things with great love.

~ Mother Teresa

❖

Intense love does not measure, it just gives.

~ Mother Teresa

❖

Love doesn't make the world go round. Love is what makes the ride worthwhile.

~ Franklin Jones

❖

A successful marriage requires falling in love many times always with the same person.

~ Mignon McLaughlin

❖

With all thy faults, I love thee still.

~ William Cowper

❖

Did my heart love till now? Forswear it, sight! For I ne'er saw true beauty till this night.

~ From Romeo and Juliet, **William Shakespeare**

❖

Love comforteth like sunshine after rain.

~ William Shakespeare

❖

Love sought is good, but given unsought is better.

~ William Shakespeare

❖

My heart is ever at your service.

~ William Shakespeare

❖

I came alive when I started loving you.

~ C.S. Lewis

❖

...she gets into the remotest recesses of my heart, and shines all through me.

~ Nathaniel Hawthorne

❖

You are the future of my past, the present of my always, the forever of my now.

~ Charles Ghigna

❖

Quotes ~ In Different Languages

Joie sans fin (*Joy without end*-French)

❖

Mon Coeur est a vous (*You have my heart*-French)

❖

Mon Amour (*My love*-French)

❖

Il mio cuore e il tuo per sempre (*My heart is yours forever*-Italian)

❖

Amore mio (*My love*-Italian)

❖

Mein Herz (*My heart*-German)

❖

Additional Ceremony Elements

Family and Friends Response

This request for response provides an opportunity for the couple's guests to participate in the ceremony by giving their verbal approval or blessing on the marriage, and typically follows the Vows.

Family and Friends Response #1

Marriage is the promise of hope between two people who love each other, who honor each other as individuals, and who wish to unite their lives and share the future together. In this ceremony, they dedicate themselves to the happiness and well being of each other, in a union of mutual caring and responsibility. Therefore, it is all the more important that those of you here with (_Groom's name_) and (_Bride's name_) may stand as witnesses to the happiness, which they have found together, and to the promises they have made to each other. As they join their lives in marriage, they also bring you together in a new relationship, creating new bonds of trust and ties of affection.

Will all of you by God's grace, do everything in your power to preserve this marriage? Will all of you, who have supported these two in friendship and love, now give your blessing upon them? If so, please show them your support by saying, "We will."

Or

Will all of you, do everything in your power to preserve this marriage? Will all of you, who have supported these two in friendship and love, now give your best wishes and support to them? If so, please show them your support by saying, "We will."

[Guests respond, "We will."]

Candle Lighting Ceremony

The Candle Lighting (also known as the lighting of the Unity candle) ceremony is most commonly performed to symbolize the joining together of the couple's individual lives into one married life. The bride and groom use two pre-lit taper candles to light a single unlit candle. Once the single candle has been lit, the taper candles may be blown out, to indicate that their two lives have been permanently merged, or they may remain lit beside the single candle, symbolizing that they now share a life and also retain their individuality. This ceremony is usually placed towards the end of the wedding ceremony.

Candle Lighting #1

(*Groom's name*) and (*Bride's name*), you may now light the Unity Candle.

(Couple lights the Unity candle)

Now you have lit a fire and that fire should not go out. The two of you now have a fire that represents love, understanding and a philosophy of life. It will give you heat, food, warmth and happiness. The new fire represents a new beginning—a new life and a new family. The fire should keep burning; for all your days together.

From every human being there arises a light that reaches straight to heaven. And when two souls that are destined to be together, find each other, their streams of light flow into a single brighter light that goes forth from their united being. May the light of love, the light of understanding, the light of respect and the light of tolerance shine eternally for both of you.

May the blessing of light, be with you always, light without and light within. And may the sun shine upon you and warm your heart until it glows like a great fire, so that others may feel the warmth of your love, for one another.

-Navajo Marriage Blessing

Candle Lighting #2

(*Groom's name*) and (*Bride's name*), your relationship was just sealed by the giving and receiving of rings. This beautiful union is symbolized through the lighting of the Unity Candle. The two distinct flames represent your lives to this moment; individual and unique. The center candle you are about to light is a candle of marriage. Its fire is magical because it represents the light of two people in love. It is a candle of Unity because both must come together, giving a spark of themselves, to create the new light. This candle is also a candle of Commitment because it takes two people working together to keep it aflame. Please light the center candle to symbolize the union of your lives.

(Couple lights the Unity candle)

As you have lit this candle today, may the brightness of the flame shine throughout your lives. May the radiance of this one light be a testimony of your unity. May this candle burn brightly as a symbol of your commitment to each other. May it give you courage and reassurance in darkness. Warmth and safety in the cold.

Rose Ceremony

Flowers historically have been used as a way of communicating one's feelings and sentiments. A single red rose has always meant, "I love you." This ceremony is a way of expressing that sentiment and honoring your new status as husband and wife. Also, long after this ceremony, each time you look at a red rose, or pass by a fragrant rose garden, you will be reminded of the love and joy that you felt on your wedding day.

Typically, the Rose Ceremony takes place at the end of the ceremony, immediately after you have been pronounced husband and wife. You begin the Rose Ceremony, by giving one another a rose. If you wish to involve children, you may also present a rose to each of them (see the "Children in the Ceremony" section of this book).

You may also extend this ceremony to others. One possibility is for the two of you to stop as you exit and hand each of your mothers your rose bud (from the Rose Ceremony), whispering "I love you," *(symbolizing that "love is not love until you give it away")*. This is a nice way of involving the mothers in the ceremony.

Throughout history lovers have sent roses to each other to express specific feelings.

Rose colors and their meanings:

- White = *Innocence*

- Yellow = *Friendship*

- Lavender = *Enchantment*

- Pink = *Joy and Gratitude*

- Coral = *Desire*

- Orange = *Fascination*

- Red = *Love and Passion*

Rose Ceremony #1

(Attendants give bride and groom each a rose)

Your gift to each other for your wedding today has been your wedding rings—which shall always be an outward demonstration of your vows of love and respect; and your commitment to each other. You now have what remains the most honorable title, which may exist between a man and a woman—the title of "husband" and "wife."

For your first gift as husband and wife, that gift will be a single rose. The rose is a symbol of love and a single rose always means one thing—the words "I love you."

Or

Your first gift to one another in your new status is a single rose, a most appropriate gift because the rose is an everlasting, enduring symbol of love and a single rose will always be a way of saying "I love you."

Please exchange your first gift as husband and wife.

(The couple exchange roses. Music may also be played at this time.)

On each anniversary of your wedding, put a single rose in your home as a reminder of the love and joy you feel today. And should day-to-day living cast any shadow over your love, be sure to place a fresh rose in your home as a peace offering and reaffirmation of the unconditional love you have for each other right now.

(Optional) As a symbol of their appreciation for their parent's love and support throughout the years, (*Bride's name*) and (*Groom's name*) will now present each of their mothers with a rose.

(The Bride and Groom each hand their mothers their roses as they exit)

Sand Ceremony

The Sand Ceremony represents leaving two separate lives and joining to make one life together. The separate lives are symbolized by two containers of sand, in different colors. The Bride and Groom come together, and pour into one vase, two individual colors of sand. Their flowing together creates a design made by the couple as they share their first experience of unity as husband and wife. The newly formed union is represented by the intertwined pattern of sand created by the couple. This symbol is then a keepsake of their wedding ceremony.

Sand Ceremony #1
(Two different colored sands are used which can be found at most arts and crafts stores. Small glass bottles or vials are usually found there as

well. A nice touch is to pour the colored sands into a "heart-shaped" bottle and later have your names and your wedding date etched on the glass bottle.)

As you each hold your sand, the separate containers represent your lives to this moment; individual and unique. As you now combine your sand together, your lives also join together as one. The life that each of you have experienced until now, individually, will hereafter be inseparably united. Just as these grains of sand can never be separated and poured again into the individual containers, so will your new life together be. You may now blend the sand together symbolizing the uniting of your individual lives in marriage.

(The bride and groom pour the two containers of sand into the third container simultaneously)

Breaking of the Glass Ceremony

The Breaking of the Glass Ceremony occurs at the end of the wedding ceremony, immediately before "the kiss," and serves to remind everyone to consider the marriage vows as an irrevocable act—just as permanent and final as the breaking of the glass is unchangeable.

Breaking of the Glass Ceremony #1

(The glass is usually a light bulb wrapped in a white towel. The best man places the glass before the groom.)

After (<u>Groom's name</u>) breaks the glass, I invite everyone to shout the Hebrew words "Mazel Tov," meaning "Good Luck" and "Congratulations."

[The groom smashes the glass with his foot and kisses the bride]

May your bond of love be as difficult to break, as it would be to put together the pieces of this glass. With congratulations, you may kiss your bride!

Wine Ceremony

In many cultures, wine symbolically represents life or spirit and the offering and accepting of wine between two people signifies a commitment to an established agreement. The wine shared by the bride and groom during a wedding ceremony symbolizes their agreement in joining their lives (by the drinking from the same "Cup of Life"), and also the recognition that like a fine wine, the relationship will mellow and get better with age.

Wine Ceremony #1

(Officiant pours wine into the goblet or chalice and holds it up)

Sip the wine of hope, toasting your lives together, recalling the many roads you have traveled, and relishing the sweet taste of anticipation in the days to come.

To friends and family gathered here today, join us in celebration; drink deep of (*Bride's name*) and (*Groom's name*)'s happiness; support them with your love.

(Officiant hands a glass to the groom, who drinks, then hands it to the bride, who drinks, and passes it back to the Officiant)

(Groom's name), Repeat after me
    I, (*Groom's name*), receive you, (*Bride's name*), as my wife; may the days ahead supply us with the finest vintages of the wine we drink today for the first time as husband and wife.

(Bride's name), Repeat after me

> I, *(Bride's name)*, receive you, *(Groom's name)*, as my husband; may the days ahead supply us with the finest vintages of the wine we drink today for the first time as husband and wife.

Wine Ceremony #2

(Officiant pours wine into the goblet or chalice and holds it up)

Bless this wine. May the sharing of this cup symbolize the sharing of your life together, with enthusiasm and delight. Let this wine represent the spirit of life. By drinking this wine now, you demonstrate your desire to blend your spirits together making your union stronger.

(Officiant hands glass to groom, who drinks, then hands it to the bride, who drinks, and passes it back to the Officiant)

(Groom's name), Repeat after me

> I drink with you, my wife, in celebration of our marriage.

(Bride's name), Repeat after me

> I drink with you, my husband, in celebration of our marriage.

Wine Ceremony #3

(Officiant pours wine into the goblet or chalice and holds it up)

The years of life are as a cup of wine poured out for you to drink. This "Cup of Life" contains within it a wine with certain properties that are sweet and symbolic of happiness, joy, hope, peace, love and delight. This same wine also holds some bitter properties that are symbolic of disappointment, sorrow, grief, despair, and life's trials and tribulations. Together the sweet and the bitter represent

"Life's Journey" and all of the experiences that are a natural part of it. Those who drink deeply from the "Cup of Life" with an open heart and willing spirit, invite the full range of challenges and experiences into their being.

This "Cup of Life" is symbolic of the pledges you have made to one another to share together the fullness of life. As you drink from this cup, you acknowledge to one another that your lives, until this moment separate, have become one. Drink now, and may the cup of your lives be sweet and full to overflowing."

(Officiant hands a glass to the groom, who drinks, then hands it to the bride, who drinks, and passes it back to the Officiant)

> As you have shared this cup of wine, so may you share your lives. May all the sweetness that it holds for you be the sweeter because you taste it together. May you find life's joys heightened, its bitterness sweetened, and all of life enriched by God's blessings upon you.

Or

> As you have shared this cup of wine, so may you share your lives. May all the sweetness that it holds for you be the sweeter because you taste it together. May you find life's joys heightened, its bitterness sweetened, and all of life enriched.

Communion Ceremony

The Communion Ceremony takes place at the end of the wedding ceremony and serves as the first act of the bride and groom as a married couple. In the Christian act of Communion the bride and the groom partake of the Bread and Cup as an expression of their marital union in Christ and faithfulness to Him.

Another more contemporary way to view the meaning of this ceremony is to recognize the embodiment of the spirit that Jesus represents. By partaking in the act of Communion the couple is inviting that spirit of the ultimate love and sacrifice into their marriage.

Communion Ceremony #1

[The Officiant passes the bread to the bride and groom]

For I received from the Lord what I also passed on to you: The Lord Jesus, on the night he was betrayed, took bread, and when he had given thanks, he broke it and said, "This is my body, which is for you; do this in remembrance of me."

[The groom serves it to the bride, the bride serves it to the groom]

[The Officiant lifts the cup and passes it to the bride and groom, they hold it between them]

In the same way, he took the cup of wine after supper, saying, "This cup is the new covenant between God and his people, an agreement confirmed with my blood. Do this to remember me as often as you drink it."

[The groom serves it to the bride, the bride serves it to the groom, the groom passes it back to the Officiant]

As you have shared this bread and cup, may you always share in the unity and peace of the Spirit.

Mother's Hawaiian Lei Presentation

The Mother's Lei Presentation ceremony provides the couple with an opportunity to demonstrate their appreciation for their mothers by presenting them with a gift representing beauty and love.

In Hawaii, Lei Aloha (Necklaces of Love) are offered and accepted open-heartedly as they give of their beauty. The lei is a welcomed celebration of one person's affection for another. The proper way to wear a lei is gently draped over the shoulders, hanging down both in front and in back. It is considered rude to remove a lei from your neck in the presence of the person who gave it to you.

Lei Presentation #1

Marriage is a coming together of two lives and a celebration of the ALOHA (love) of two people. But it is more. The love that (*Groom's name*) and (*Bride's name*) feel for one another is the flowering of a seed their parents planted in their hearts years ago. As they embrace one another in their love, so do they embrace the families that have been brought together on this happy occasion. As a sign of their love for their families, they would like to offer these symbols of eternal ALOHA, these leis, to their mothers, (*Groom's mom's name*) and (*Bride's mom's name*).

(*Couple presents the leis to each mother, placing the lei around each one's neck and kissing them on each cheek.*)

Lei Aloha (Necklaces of Love)—are offered and accepted open-heartedly as they give of their beauty. (*Groom's mom's name*) and (*Bride's mom's name*) may these leis embrace your thoughts, your senses and your hearts. These leis are a promise that no matter how far apart you are that you are not forgotten and a reminder that you are always in their hearts and prayers.

Hawaiian Lei Exchange

The Lei Exchange between the Bride and Groom may occur at the end of the wedding ceremony as the couple's first act as husband and wife. Or, this exchange could occur at the beginning of the ceremony in place of the Dedication Blessing.

In Hawaii, the lei is a traditional "Makana"—a gift exchanged between bride and groom. Lei Aloha (Necklaces of Love)—are offered and accepted open-heartedly as they give of their beauty. The lei is a welcomed celebration of one person's affection for another. The proper way to wear a lei is gently draped over the shoulders, hanging down both in front and in back. It is considered rude to remove a lei from your neck in the presence of the person who gave it to you.

Lei Exchange #1

(Officiant to the Groom)
Please repeat after me, in Hawaiian:
Lei no, au ko, aloha—Please wear my love, like a beautiful lei. Now place the lei around the neck of your beloved and give her a kiss on each cheek.

(Groom places the lei around the Bride's neck)

(Officiant to the Bride)

Please repeat after me, in Hawaiian:

Lei no, au ko, aloha—Please wear my love, like a beautiful lei. Now place the lei around the neck of your beloved and give him a kiss on each cheek.

(Bride places the lei around the Groom's neck)

As your Aloha for one another, may these leis embrace your thoughts, your senses and your hearts.

Butterfly Release Ceremony

Butterflies may be released to symbolize wishes or blessings to be fulfilled for the marriage. During this ceremony, a wish or blessing is stated, or guests are asked to silently make a wish for the couple and then the butterflies are released. This signifies their wishes or blessings, being carried on the wings of the butterflies into the heavens to be granted. This ceremony is commonly placed toward the end of the wedding ceremony.

Butterfly Release #1

(A small package containing one butterfly is placed under each guest's chair prior to the beginning of the ceremony)

Marriage is a venture of faith. It is a life of loving, comforting, honoring and keeping. (*Groom's name*) and (*Bride's name*) bring to this venture their unique history, personality and spirit. Part of their history was shared with friends and family who have passed on. (*Groom's name*) and (*Bride's name*) would like to create a special memory to express the union of marriage and for those who have touched their lives. There is an Indian Legend regarding the release of butterflies and as the Indian Legend Goes;

If anyone desires a wish to come true they must first capture a butterfly and whisper that wish to it.

Since a butterfly can make no sound, the butterfly cannot reveal the wish to anyone but the Great Spirit who hears and sees all.

In gratitude for giving the beautiful butterfly its freedom, the Great Spirit always grants the wish.

So, according to legend, by making a wish and giving the butterfly its freedom, the wish will be taken to the heavens and be granted.

Today we have gathered to grant this couple all our best wishes and are about to set these butterflies free in the trust that all these wishes will be granted.

Please look under your chair for the box enclosing the butterfly. At the end of the song, please join (_Bride's name_) and (_Groom's name_) in releasing their best wishes.

(Song Plays)

Butterfly Release #2

(A small package containing one butterfly is placed under each guest's chair prior to the beginning of the ceremony)

And now (_Bride's name_) and (_Groom's name_) would like you to join them in a Butterfly Release Ceremony.

May the wings of the butterfly kiss the sun
And find your shoulder to light on,
To bring you luck, happiness and riches
Today, tomorrow and beyond.

–Irish Blessing

Please look under your chair for the box enclosing the butterfly. At the end of the song, please join (_Bride's name_) and (_Groom's name_) in releasing their best wishes.
(Song Plays)

Dove Release Ceremony

The ceremonial releasing of doves has been a custom for centuries. Doves choose one partner for life and make this commitment until death. The white dove has been used throughout history as a symbol of Love, Peace, Purity, Faithfulness and Prosperity. The release of the doves traditionally occurs at the end of the wedding ceremony (either after the Closing Blessing, or in place of the Closing Blessing).

Most organizations that provide the birds actually use pure white homing pigeons (instead of doves). The reason for this is that releasing little white doves means certain death for these creatures, not only because they cannot find their way home, but because they are unable to defend themselves against predators or find food in the wild. They are nervous little birds, not strong flyers, and when released at your event, will invariably land on the ground or a nearby perch in one big, disappointing plop. So, to ensure a spectacular, release of birds guaranteed to fly and delight the crowd as they circle overhead before disappearing into the distance, make certain that pure white homing pigeons are used in your release. After they are released, nature enables them to find their way home (to their handlers) from hundreds of miles. And a release is always scheduled early enough in the day to allow them to get home, fed and be safely on their perches before sunset.

Dove Release Ceremony #1

The white dove has been used throughout history as a symbol of love, peace, purity, faithfulness and prosperity. Doves also choose one partner for life.

At this time, _____ and _____ please release the doves to represent the love and commitment you have given to one another this day.

(The couple opens the cage to release the doves)
From this day forward, whenever you see a white dove, may you be reminded of this moment and the commitment you have made to each other.

Hand Blessing Ceremony

Hands are believed to be a connection to the heart, and the joining of hands symbolically unites two hearts. The Hand Blessing (also known as "Blessing of the Hands") ceremonially signifies the bond of the heart in the promises being made between the bride and groom. This ceremony is commonly placed just before the exchange of rings.

Hand Blessing Ceremony #1

(*Bride's name*), please hold (*Groom's name*) hands palms up, so you may see the gift that they are to you.

These are the hands of your best friend, young and strong and vibrant with love, that are holding yours on your wedding day, as he promises to passionately love you and cherish you through the years, for a lifetime of happiness.

These are the hands that will work along side yours, as together you build your future, as you laugh and cry, as you share your innermost secrets and dreams.

These are the hands that will countless times wipe the tears from your eyes: tears of sorrow and tears of joy.

These are the hands that will comfort you in illness, and hold you when fear or grief engulfs your heart.

These are the hands that when wrinkled and aged will still

be reaching for yours, still giving you the same unspoken tenderness with just a touch.

These are the hands that will tenderly lift your chin and brush your cheek as they raise your face to look into his eyes: eyes that are filled completely with his overwhelming love and desire for you.

Optional Humor: At this point while the groom's hands are still on top, the Officiant asks the groom to take a good long look at the position of his hands. As the groom looks down at his hands the Officiant says, "Because this is the last time you will have the upper hand."

(*Groom's name*), please hold (*Bride's name*) hands palms up, so you may see the gift that they are to you.

These are the hands of your best friend, smooth, young and carefree, that are holding yours on your wedding day, as she promises to passionately love you and cherish you through the years, for a lifetime of happiness.

These are the hands that will massage tension from your neck and back in the evenings after you've both had a long hard day.

These are the hands that will hold you tight as you struggle through difficult times.

These are the hands that will comfort you when you are sick, or console you when you are grieving.

These are the hands that when wrinkled and aged will still be reaching for yours, still giving you the same unspoken tenderness with just a touch.

These are the hands that will give you support as she encourages you to pursue your dreams.

Together, everything you wish for can be realized.

God, bless these hands that you see before you this day. May they always be held by one another. Give them the strength to hold on during the storms of stress and the darkness of disillusionment. Keep them tender and gentle as they nurture each other in their wondrous love. Help these hands to continue building a relationship founded in your grace, rich in caring, and devoted in reaching for your perfection. May (_Groom's name_) and (_Bride's name_) see their four hands as healer, protector, shelter and guide. We ask this in (Your/Jesus) name, Amen.

Or

May these hands be blessed that we see before us this day. May they always be held by one another. May they have the strength to hold on during the storms of stress and the darkness of disillusionment. May they remain tender and gentle as they nurture each other in their wondrous love. May these hands continue building a relationship founded in love, rich in caring, and devoted in reaching for perfection. May (_Groom's name_) and (_Bride's name_) see their four hands as healer, protector, shelter and guide.

Celtic Hand-Fasting Ceremony

Hand-fasting was traditionally a very simple ceremony where the bride and groom faced each other and joined right hand to right hand and left hand to left hand and were bound by a ceremonial wrap or rope to signify their union in marriage. The expression "tying the knot" came from this Celtic marriage ritual. The Hand-fasting may be used in place of the Declaration of Intent, used as the conclusion of the ceremony, or serve as the complete wedding ceremony.

Hand-Fasting Ceremony #1

(_Bride's name_) and (_Groom's name_) have chosen to incorporate the ancient Celtic ritual of Hand-fasting into their wedding ceremony today. Hand-fasting is a declaration of intent, where the couple clearly state that they are marrying of their own free will.

(*Bride's name*) and (*Groom's name*), know now before you go further, that since your lives have crossed in this life, you have formed eternal and sacred bonds. As you seek to enter this state of matrimony you should strive to make real the ideals that give meaning to this ceremony and to the sanctity of marriage. With full awareness, know that within this circle you are not only declaring your intent to be hand-fasted before your friends and family, but you speak that intent also to God.

The promises made today and the ties that are bound here greatly strengthen your union and will cross the years and lives of each soul's growth.

Do you seek to enter this ceremony? (*Couple answers, "Yes"*)

(*Bride's name*) and (*Groom's name*), please look into each other's eyes.
[*Couple holds hands – Bride's left hand, Groom's right hand*]

Will you honor and respect one another, and seek to never break that honor? (*Couple answers, "We will"*)
[*The first cord is draped over the couple's hands*]

Will you share each other's pain and seek to ease it? (*Couple answers, "We will"*)
[*The second cord is draped over the couple's hands*]

Will you share the burdens of each so that your spirits may grow in this union? (*Couple answers, "We will"*)
[*The third cord is draped over the couple's hands*]

Will you share each other's laughter, and look for the brightness in life and the positive in each other? (*Couple answers, "We will"*)
[*Fourth cord is draped over the couple's hands and then the cords are tied together*]

(*Bride's name*) and (*Groom's name*), as your hands are bound together now, so your lives and spirits are joined in a union of love and trust. The bond of this marriage is not formed by these cords, but rather by the vows you have made. For always you hold in your own hands the fate of this union. Above you are the stars and below you is the earth. Like the stars your love should be a constant source of light, and like the earth, a firm foundation from which to grow.

God, bless these hands that you see before you this day. May they always be held by one another. Give them the strength to hold on during the storms of stress and the darkness of disillusionment. Keep them tender and gentle as they nurture each other in their wondrous love. Help these hands to continue building a relationship founded in your grace, rich in caring, and devoted in reaching for your perfection. May (_Bride's name_) and (_Groom's name_) see their hands as healer, protector, shelter and guide. We ask this in (Your name/Jesus), Amen.

Or

May these hands be blessed that we see before us this day. May they always be held by one another. May they have the strength to hold on during the storms of stress and the darkness of disillusionment. May they remain tender and gentle as they nurture each other in their wondrous love. May these hands continue building a relationship founded in love, rich in caring, and devoted in reaching for perfection. May (_Bride's name_) and (_Groom's name_) see their hands as healer, protector, shelter and guide.

(_Officiant unties the cords_)

Hand-Fasting Ceremony #2

(*Bride's name*) and (*Groom's name*), please look into each other's eyes.

Will you honor and respect one another, and seek to never break that honor? (*Couple answers, "We will"*)
  [*The first cord is draped over the couple's hands*]
And so the binding is made.

Will you share each other's pain and seek to ease it? (*Couple answers, "We will"*)
  [*The second cord is draped over the couple's hands*]

And so the binding is made.

Will you share the burdens of each so that your spirits may grow in this union? (*Couple answers, "We will"*)
  [*The third cord is draped over the couple's hands*]

And so the binding is made.

Will you share each other's laughter, and look for the brightness in life and the positive in each other? (*Couple answers, "We will"*)
  [*The forth cord is draped over the couple's hands*]

And so the binding is made.

[*Officiant ties the cords together*]
  (*Bride's name*) and (*Groom's name*), as your hands are bound together now, so your lives and spirits are joined in a union of love and trust. Above you are the stars and below you is the earth. Like the stars your love should be a constant source of light, and like the earth, a firm foundation from which to grow.

(Officiant unties the cords)

God, bless these hands that you see before you this day. May they always be held by one another. Give them the strength to hold on during the storms of stress and the darkness of disillusionment. Keep them tender and gentle as they nurture each other in their wondrous love. Help these hands to continue building a relationship founded in your grace, rich in caring, and devoted in reaching for your perfection. May (*Bride's name*) and (*Groom's name*) see their hands as healer, protector, shelter and guide. We ask this in (Your name/Jesus), Amen.

Or

May these hands be blessed that we see before us this day. May they always be held by one another. May they have the strength to hold on during the storms of stress and the darkness of disillusionment. May they remain tender and gentle as they nurture each other in their wondrous love. May these hands continue building a relationship founded in love, rich in caring, and devoted in reaching for perfection. May (*Bride's name*) and (*Groom's name*) see their hands as healer, protector, shelter and guide.

Celtic Trinity Ceremony

The Celtic trinity is an ancient profession of faith which maintains that trust in the soul (demonstrated in the drinking of the ale or wine), belief in the heart (demonstrated in the binding of the hands with rope) and faith in the mind (demonstrated in the lighting of the candles) are all that is needed to lead an honorable, loving and fulfilled life. This ceremony is commonly placed just prior to the ring exchange or at the end of the wedding ceremony.

Celtic Trinity Ceremony #1

(*Bride's name*) and (*Groom's name*), in marriage, your souls will join together so that your strengths shall be twice as great and your hardships will be only half as difficult.

[Officiant pours the ale or wine into the cup]

As you share the (ale/wine) from this wedding cup let it remind you to trust in your soul which is the Universal spirit. Trust in its strength and it will strengthen the bond between you.

[Officiant hands the cup to the bride, who takes a sip and hands it to the groom, who takes a sip, and hands it back to the Officiant]

[Officiant then holds up the silk rope]

Please place your hands over one another.

Your open hands placed over one another represent your hearts, the silk rope represents the belief which binds them together.

Belief in your heart is a testament to the power of love and compassion. Belief in the heart is the constant desire to put your spouse before you in every way, to act mindful and to allow love and patience to prevail. Belief in your heart will always guide your marriage and allow the power of love to grow, multiply and strengthen. At times, your souls may drift apart, but the belief in your heart will act as a silk tether, which will keep you together.

[Officiant then binds together their hands by wrapping the silk rope around them]

Having faith in your mind is the last concept of the Celtic trinity. May each of you maintain your independence of mind, respecting each other's thoughts and trying to learn from one another. May positive thoughts always guide you.

[Officiant lights the candles]

These candles represent the light that burns away the darkness of ignorance. May you always strive to keep your mind bright, sharp and uncluttered. Your mindfulness will add joy and ease to your marriage.

Jumping the Broom or Branch Ceremony

The broom or branch represents a threshold (a place or point of new venture). The couple, although still individuals, are beginning a new life together as a couple. Jumping over the broom or branch represents crossing this threshold into new territory, a life genuinely connected to another's. The leap that the couple takes over the broom or branch is also symbolic of the fact that starting a new life with another person does require a "leap of faith." By taking the leap, the individuals make a gesture of dedication to working together through the challenges ahead. This ceremony is commonly placed at the end of the wedding ceremony.

Jumping the Broom or Branch Ceremony #1

[Officiant holds up the broom or branch]

It is tradition to jump over a (broom/branch) together to finalize the marriage. This symbolizes the transition into a new existence where you are committed to each other and to a life of growth and love.
[Officiant places the broom or branch on the ground]

(*Groom's name*) and (*Bride's name*), please join hands now and jump over the (broom/branch) into your new life together.

[The couple jumps over the broom or branch]

Invoking the Four Directions Ceremony

The purpose of this ceremony is to receive blessings for the marriage from the energy or spirit of the four directions. In some cultures it is believed that the human soul shares characteristics with all things divine. It is this belief, which has assigned elements and virtues to each of the four cardinal directions from which to receive blessings. East is the element Air, for openness and breath, communication of the heart, and purity of the mind and body. South is the element Fire, for energy, passion, creativity and the warmth of a loving home. West is the element Water, for capacity to feel emotion. And North is the element Earth, which provides sustenance, fertility and security. This ceremony is commonly placed at the end of the wedding ceremony as a closing blessing.

Invoking the Four Directions Ceremony #1

It is believed that the human soul shares characteristics with all things divine. It is according to this belief that we now align ourselves with the four cardinal directions and their associated elements. Each of these blessings emphasizes that which will help you build a happy and successful union.

[Guests are invited to stand and face the East]
Please stand and join (*Bride's name*) and (*Groom's name*) as they face the East.

Blessed be this union with the gifts of the East and the element of Air, for openness and breath, communication of the heart, and purity of the mind and body. From the east you receive the gift of a new beginning with the rising of each Sun, and the understanding that each day is a new opportunity for growth.

[Guests are invited to face the South]
Please face the South.

Blessed be this union with the gifts of the South and the element of Fire, for energy, passion, creativity and the warmth of a loving home. From the fire within you generate light, which you will share with one another in even the darkest of times.

[Guests are invited to face the West]
Please face the West.

Blessed be this union with the gifts of the West, the element of Water, for capacity to feel emotion.

In marriage you offer absolute trust to one another, and vow to keep your hearts open in sorrow as well as joy.

[Guests are invited to face the North]
Please face the North.

Blessed be this union with the gifts of the North, the element of Earth, which provides sustenance, fertility and security. The earth will feed and enrich you, and help you to build a stable home to which you may always return.

[Guests are invited to face the altar]

Go now, with the blessings and support of those you love and those who love you.

Children in the Ceremony

Including your children in the ceremony provides an opportunity for a commitment to be made between a child and a new parent, where the new parent vows to accept the child, and the child vows to accept the new parent and the established parent vows to support the relationship.

Vows with Children

Something that is becoming more common is to include children in a family vow after the bride and groom's vows. For example, "I, (*Parent's name*), solemnly promise that I will care for you, love you and honor you." (Some people also give a small medallion or piece of jewelry, saying something like, "Take this as a symbol of our family, and our love for you.")

Or, during the "I Do's" … the child is asked if they agree to love, honor and support the family relationship and they answer "I Do." The child may also place their hand on top of the couple's clasped hands during this part of the ceremony.

Examples of vows with children:

(*Child's name*), I receive you as my (son/daughter). I promise to always love you and support you, to hold you close and watch over you forever and always.

❖

(*Child's name*), I promise to be there for you when you need me, to support you in all that you do. I thank you for being the wonderful (son/daughter/children) that you are.
(*Child's name*), I offer this gift as a token of my promise to you, that I will always be committed to you as a loving parent.

❖

(*Child's name*), I give this (ring/necklace/gift) to you as a symbol of my promise, to love you, support you, guide you, and believe in you always.

❖

This (ring/medallion) is round, symbolizing that love is a circle, a circle that is meant to include those it encounters. I give this to you (*Child's name*) as a pledge to always include you in the love I have for your (mother/father). Please accept this ring as a symbol of our new family.

❖

(*Child's name*), I promise you before our family and friends, that I will be a loving parent. I welcome you into my heart and home.

❖

(*Child's name*), I promise you before God, our family and friends, that I will be a loving parent. I welcome you into my heart and home.

❖

(*Child's name*), I promise to protect and love you all of my life. I will do my best to guide and support you.

❖

Flower Ceremony with Children

(The bride, groom and children are each given a single flower to place in a vase at the altar.)

The two of you are combining your strengths and hopes in this marriage. Your decision to marry will also shape and deeply affect the lives of (*Children's names*). All of you will touch each other in a special way from now on. Today we are acknowledging both the creation of a marriage and the creation of a family. Each of you will contribute your individual flowers to this new relationship, combining your unique selves into a bouquet that is more rich and varied than any of you could create by yourselves. I ask you now to symbolize the wonder and beauty of the beginning of this new family by each offering your flower to create a single bouquet (*each puts a flower into the vase*). Together may your new family be happy.

Blended Family Ceremony

It is the desire of (*Bride's name*) and (*Groom's name*) to extend their commitments to each other by making promises to the children of this family. As you all join hands to form a new circle of love, we will seal this union with spoken promises like the rings this bride and groom have exchanged.

Do you (*Bride's name*) and (*Groom's name*), promise to be faithful, loving, tender and nurturing parents, always there for (*Children's names*), providing for (their/her/his) physical needs, and for (their/her/his) emotional needs, always being a good listener, a loving counselor and a friend?

(Bride & Groom respond) We do.

Repeat after me:

(*Bride's/Groom's name*) I want you to know that I love your (mother/father) very much. I promise you my trust, fairness and support. I promise to share my knowledge, to be your friend, and to provide a shoulder to cry on. I promise to be available to you, as I am to your (mother/father).

(Bride or Groom to each Child) (*Child's name*), I give you this (*gift/necklace/ring, etc.*) as a sign of my loving promises made this day.

(Officiant to the Children) Do you accept these promises made by (*Bride's/Groom's name*)?

(Child or Children respond) (I do/We do).

(Officiant says) May God now bless you all as a family, and bless this marriage.

Or

(*Officiant says*) We wish the best for you all as a family, and this marriage.

Sand Ceremony with Children

The Sand Ceremony represents leaving separate lives and joining to make one life together. The separate lives are symbolized by three or more containers of sand, in different colors. The Bride, Groom and children come together, and pour into one vase, their individual colors of sand. Their flowing together creates a design as they share their first experience of unity as a family. The newly formed union is represented by the intertwined pattern of sand created by the family. This symbol is then a keepsake of the wedding ceremony.

Three or more (depending on how many children are participating) different colored sands are used which can be found at most arts and crafts stores. Small glass bottles or vials are usually found there as well. (A nice touch is to pour the colored sands into a "heart-shaped" bottle and later have your names and your wedding date etched on the glass bottle).

Words spoken: As you each hold your sand, the separate containers represent your lives to this moment; individual and unique. As you now combine your sand together, your lives also join together as one family. The life that each of you have experienced until now, individually, will hereafter be inseparably united. Just as these grains of sand can never be separated and poured again into the individual containers, so will your new life together be. You may now blend the sand together symbolizing the uniting of your family.

(The bride, groom and children pour their containers of sand into the empty container simultaneously.)

❖

Ring or Necklace Ceremony with Children

A ring or necklace is placed on the child, and words are spoken by the new parent about uniting them as a family. Or both parents place the necklace or ring on the child and ask for the child's approval of the union. (See "Vows with Children" in this section for examples of words to use with this ceremony)

Ribbon Ceremony with Children

This ceremony may be placed just before the pronouncement of marriage. The children of the bride or groom approach the couple and loosely bind their clasped hands together at the wrist with ribbon to symbolize their support of the union. No words need to be spoken at this time. Or you may have the Officiant say some words about the significance of this symbolic gesture. Example: "(Children's names), (has/have) now demonstrated (his/her/their) support of this union."

Rose Ceremony with Children

Typically, the Rose Ceremony takes place at the end of the ceremony, immediately after you have been pronounced husband and wife. You may include this ceremony after the couple's Rose Ceremony, or use this ceremony by itself.

Sample Rose Ceremony with Children:

(Attendants give bride and groom each a rose)

As a symbol of their love for their (daughter/son/children),

(*Bride's name*) and (*Groom's name*) will now present (*Children's names*) [each] with a rose as their first act as a married couple.

(*The Bride and Groom will hand each of the children a rose bud, whispering "I love you," before proceeding with their exit, knowing that love is not love until you give it away. This is a nice way of involving the children in the ceremony.*)

Honoring Parents

Including parents in the ceremony provides an opportunity for the couple to give recognition and communicate gratitude to those who were essential in the development of the bride and groom's values that has led them to this moment.

Examples for honoring parents:

(*Words to the Bride's/Groom's parents*)
(*Bride or Groom's Parent's names*), please stand. (*Bride's/Groom's name*) thanks you for raising (*Bride's/Groom's name*) to be the (man/woman) of (his/her) dreams. (He/She) thanks you for the love and care, which has made (him/her) so special. (*Bride's/Groom's name*) asks you now to accept (her/him) as your (daughter/son). And, thanks you for raising (*Bride's/Groom's name*) to be the (man/woman) (he/she) chooses to spend (his/her) life with.

Before (*Bride's name*) and (*Groom's name*) say their vows, they want to thank their parents for all that they have done for them. They learned how to love because they were raised in loving homes. They feel secure and confident in their love because their parents allowed them to be independent. Their parents are their support and have shown them by example, what a happy marriage can be. And for this, they thank you.

❖

(*Bride's name*) and (*Groom's name*) thank everyone for coming today. Your presence makes this ceremony more meaningful for them. They especially want to thank their parents—not just for being here today, but for being there for them so many times in the past. Although they are establishing a new home, the love they feel for the homes of their childhood will continue.

❖

Remembrance

The Remembrance gives the bride and groom an opportunity to honor and remember loved ones who are unable to attend the wedding ceremony.

Examples for remembering loved ones:

At this time, we would like to honor the memory of (*Groom's/Bride's name*)'s grandparents, (*Grandparent's names*), who, while no longer with us physically, are carried in our hearts.

❖

At this time, we would like to honor the memory of (*Groom's/Bride's name*)'s (grandmother/grandfather), (*Grandmother's/Grandfather's name*), who is here today in our hearts.

❖

At this time, we would like to honor the memory of (*Groom's/Bride's name*)'s (mother/father), (*Mother's/Father's name*), who, while unable to be here today, is carried in our hearts.

❖

(*Groom's name*) and (*Bride's name*) have asked that we take a moment to honor the memory of those loved ones who could not be with us today, but are here today in spirit.

❖

There are two special people, (*Loved one's name*) and (*Loved one's name*), who are unable to be here with us today, so let us remember them in our hearts.

❖

Remembrance with candle-lighting:

Marriage is a venture of faith. It is a life of loving, comforting, honoring and keeping. (*Groom's name*) and (*Bride's name*) bring to this venture their unique history, personality and spirit. Part of their history was shared with their parents who have passed on. In memory of their lives and spirits, they light these candles in our midst, in celebration of this marriage.

(Groom lights candle)   (<u>*Groom's name*</u>) will now light a candle,
In memory of (<u>*Parent's names*</u>)

(Bride lights candle)   (<u>*Bride's name*</u>) will now light a candle,
In memory of (<u>*Parent's names*</u>)

❖

Music in the Ceremony

Music has the power to set a mood, evoke emotion, and enhance the significance of a moment. Traditionally, music is played for the Prelude (when your guests are finding seats and waiting for the ceremony to begin), during the Procession, Recession and Postlude (when your guests are exiting, and/or waiting in the receiving line). Music may be placed anywhere in the ceremony, for example, after the vows, during a Candle Lighting Ceremony (or any additional ceremonial element), or in place of a reading.

There are many choices for the method of including music in your ceremony, such as; songs played by a Disc Jockey (DJ), a solo sung by a friend, songs played by a harpist, songs played by a string quartet, songs played by your favorite local band. These methods can also be combined; for example, you could have a harpist play during the prelude and postlude and have a DJ play songs during the ceremony.

If you are designing a more traditional ceremony, you may want to select the traditional Wagner's "Here Comes the Bride" for the Bride's walk down the aisle and Pachelbel's "Canon in D" for the rest of the wedding party's walk down the aisle. Or if you are designing a more contemporary ceremony, you may want to select a song that captures your personality like Norah Jones' "Come Away with Me" for the Bride's walk down the aisle.

The following is a small sample of both classic and contemporary wedding ceremony music. Many of the songs can be used for processionals and recessionals, or serve as prelude or postlude music.

Traditional Wedding Ceremony Music

- "Bridal Chorus from Lohengrin" (Richard Wagner) (also known as "Here Comes the Bride")

- "Canon in D" (Johann Pachelbel)

- "Guitar Concerto in D Major," Largo, (Antonio Vivaldi)

- "Air" (from Water Music Suite), (George Frederic Handel)

- "The Prince of Denmark's March" (Trumpet Voluntary in D major) (Jeremiah Clarke)

- "Procession of Joy" (Hal Hopson)

- "Rigaudon" (Andre Campra)

- "Wedding March" (from The Marriage of Figaro), (Wolfgang Amadeus Mozart)

- Prelude from "Te Deum" (Marc-Antoine Charpentier)

- "Trumpet Tune and Air" (Henry Purcell)

- "Trumpet Voluntary" (John Stanley)

Other Classical Wedding Ceremony Music

- "Coronation March for Czar Alexander III" (Peter I. Tchaikovsky)

- "Overture" (from Royal Fireworks Music), (George Frederic Handel)

- "Promenade" (from Pictures at an Exhibition), (Modest Mussorgsky)

- "Sinfonia" (from Cantata No. 156), (Johann Sebastian. Bach)

- "Cantata No.29" (Johann Sebastian Bach)

- "Prelude and Fugue in C" (Johann Sebastian Bach)

- "Toccata" (from L'Orfeo), (Claudio Monteverdi)

- "Romance from String Quartet" (Wolfgang Amadeus Mozart)

- "Piano Concerto No. 21 in C major" ("Elvira Madigan") (Wolfgang Amadeus Mozart)

- "Trumpet Tune in A-Major" (David N. Johnson)

- "A Midsummer Night's Dream, incidental music, Op. 61 Wedding March" (Felix Mendelssohn)

- "Winter," Largo or "Spring" Allegro (from The Four Seasons), (Antonio Vivaldi)

Contemporary Songs for Wedding Ceremonies

- "At Last" (Etta James)

- "Only Time" (Enya)

- "Come Away With Me" (Norah Jones)

- "Appalachia Waltz" (Yo-Yo Ma, Edgar Meyer, Mark O'Connor)

- "Unforgettable" (Nat King Cole and Natalie Cole)

- "The Look of Love" (Dionne Warwick/Burt Bacharach)

- "The Vow" (Jeremy Lubbock)

- "Come What May" (Nicole Kidman and Ewan McGregor)

- "Storybook Love" from the movie "The Princess Bride" (Willy DeVille)

- "Wedding Processional" (from The Sound of Music) (Richard Rodgers & Oscar Hammerstein)

- "Can't Help Falling in Love" (Elvis Presley)

- "What A Wonderful World" (Louis Armstrong)

- "When I'm Sixty-Four" (The Beatles)

- "In My Life" (The Beatles)

There are many options for including music in your ceremony and ultimately the choices you make should reflect the personalities of the two of you.

Ideas for Personalizing
Your Wedding Ceremony

Include a favorite flower, candle, picture, or special object for a parent, sibling or any other close person, who is unable to attend the wedding, to symbolize their presence in spirit.

. Have a friend read a passage from the bible, a poem, a short story, lyrics of a song, or a favorite writing that has special meaning for the couple. Have the Best Man read something he wrote or selected for the Groom, and have the Maid or Matron of Honor read something she wrote or selected for the Bride.

Pick flowers together from a field of wild flowers, to use as decorations or for the bouquets.

❖

Have a small private wedding with family and just a few close friends, and save the big gathering for the reception.

❖

Invite a friend with a musical talent to perform a special song, play the flute, guitar, etc. or sing. Possibly have them write and perform a special song for the couple.

❖

As people arrive or during the reception, show a slideshow or video of the bride and groom as children, through the years as individuals and as a couple. Try to find a few funny ones to promote laughter.

❖

Involve your guests in the ceremony, ask people to volunteer to say something about the couple, share a story or say a prayer.

❖

Have the ceremony at a special time of day; Sunrise, Sunset, Dusk, Dawn or nighttime under the stars.

❖

Have the ceremony at a special time of year or on a Holiday that has meaning for the two of you. Examples: Winter, Spring, Summer,

Fall, New Years Eve at Midnight—the new year begins the new life of the couple (countdown to the kiss).

Instead of throwing birdseed or blowing bubbles, give each guest a small brass bell to ring as you leave for your honeymoon. The guests can keep the bells as a Christmas ornament to remember your wedding.

Instead of gifts for the couple, have a gift exchange. Have guests bring a gift (set a price limit) to be exchanged with other guests during the reception.

Pick seasonal berries together to be eaten at the reception.

Collect leaves together for decorating the wedding with a Fall theme. Toss leaves along the path the couple will walk, bringing the leaves indoors to give an outdoors feeling.

Supply each guest with a candle and at the conclusion of the ceremony, have the groomsmen light the candles to stay lit for the duration of a prayer or reading of a special passage.

Have the ceremony somewhere in nature:

- On the beach, barefoot in the sand

- In a field of wildflowers

- In the woods

- On a mountain in the snow

- By a river, with the sound of the flowing water in the background

❖

Top the wedding cake with a tiny sapling. Then the tree can be planted at the couple's home, so that they can watch it grow as their marriage grows.

❖

Light a different colored candle for each of the qualities you want to strengthen your marriage:

- WHITE - Purity, Truth, Sincerity
- RED - Strength, Health, Vigor, Intimate Love
- LIGHT BLUE - Tranquility, Understanding, Patience, Health
- GREEN - Finance, Fertility, Luck
- GOLD or YELLOW - Attraction, Persuasion, Charm, Confidence

- PINK - Honor, Love, Morality
- ORANGE - Encouragement, Adaptability, Stimulation, Attraction

Use scent to create a mood:

- Lavender - relaxing, reduces stress
- Cinnamon - elevates mood, relieves fatigue
- Lemon - cools and refreshes, energizing and purifying
- Orange - calming, cooling and refreshing, stimulates optimism and humor
- Peppermint - energizing, cooling
- Rosemary - enhances mental clarity, concentration, memory, and creativity

Make a time capsule. Write down your hopes and dreams in letters to each other. Then put them in a box, along with a favorite bottle of wine and a few memorable items. Open this on your 10th anniversary.

Have a special wedding quilt that will be signed on one side by all of your friends and family during the reception. Every time you sleep with it you will remember your beautiful wedding.

Request that your guests bring to the wedding a small Christmas ornament (1 per family) from their personal collections. This is to remember all of your friends and family who came to your wedding. Hang up all the little ornaments they gave to you on your tree at Christmas.

❖

Instead of a Guest book, have an engraving tool available for your guests to sign their names on an engravable tray.

❖

Have guests sign a tablecloth with a fabric pen. Later, have the names embroidered. The tablecloth can then be used on each anniversary.

❖

Place an invitation or photo of the couple in the center of a piece of poster board. Have your guests sign around the invitation or photo. This can be framed later and hung in your home.

❖

Have each usher give a flower to each female guest as they arrive for the ceremony.

Have someone take candid photos of each guest with the bride and groom to be later sent to the guest in their Thank you card.

❖

Have a post-wedding party at your home after the honeymoon. This is a great way to show off your wedding photographs and video and to use some of the wonderful gifts you received.

❖

If far-away relatives cannot be with you for your wedding, have them record a message that you can play at the reception, allowing them to deliver their best wishes in their own voices, or include them "live" via video-conference on a mobile computer.

❖

For an unusual wedding favor keepsake that helps others—consider donating the money allotted for wedding favors to a favorite charity, and placing certificates at each place-setting, rolled up and tied with a delicate ribbon, that declare a donation made in the name of each guest.

❖

Animal lovers might place origami animals at each table setting instead of wedding favors, with a declaration that a donation was made to the local animal shelter or a wild animal "adopted."

❖

To create a wedding scrapbook, have a bridesmaid and groomsman circulate among the guests taking candid pictures of them and giving them small note cards to write a message to go with the picture. Later paste each picture onto a page in a scrapbook and add the note cards with the guest's thoughts below their photo.

Have a garden wedding complete with bridesmaids in romantic, flower-strewn, wide-brimmed hats. For a relaxed, informal wedding, buy plain, matching straw hats, then have a hat-decorating party with your bridesmaids. Supply a variety of beautiful ribbons, silk flowers, beads, feathers, and pins. Your bridesmaids will have a lot of fun and great memories, and they'll cherish their unique keepsakes.

Let each of your bridesmaids choose her favorite flower, or designate one to her, so that each bouquet is unique. Your bridal bouquet could be composed of all the different flowers. Each groomsman's boutonnière could match the bouquet of the bridesmaid he will be escorting down the aisle.

Place a colorful square of cloth at each reception table place-setting and a few fabric pens on each table. Ask guests to sign the squares, and then use them to create a one-of-a-kind wedding wish quilt.

Spread your wedding joy further by donating your centerpieces after the reception. Floral arrangements will be gratefully received at nursing homes and hospitals.

Update the tradition of having all the guests sign the Guest Book as witnesses by inviting them to sign a calligraphic poster of your wedding vows.

Nature enthusiasts might consider a woodland-inspired ring pillow, made of plump tufts of moss placed on a small tray and trimmed with ivy and flowers.

For a father who has passed on, the bride may write or choose a poem to remember him and record her voice reciting the poem with soft music behind it. As she walks down the aisle it is a tribute to him and a way of including him in the ceremony.

Reserve the back page of the wedding programs for thank-yous and a letter to dad or mom. For example, "Hi Dad … I wish you could be here to walk me down the aisle. With Love, from your daughter, Laura."

Present flowers to the mothers or grandmothers. After the bride walks down the aisle, she may present a single flower of her choice to her mother or grandmothers and her finance's mother or grandmothers. Attach a note to each flower stating the importance of them in your lives.

After the ceremony, ask all of the guests to linger for a group photo that will later be used as the cover for the your thank-you cards.

Have each guest pick up a small stone before the ceremony that you have hand-selected from meaningful places—where the two of you met, where you live now, the wedding location, etc. Ask your guests to hold the stones during the ceremony and make a special wish. At the end of the ceremony, instruct your guests to deposit the stones into a large glass container for you to display in your home.

Sample Ceremonies

Civil Ceremony

Welcome

We have come here today, to celebrate and support the choice of (*Bride's name*) and (*Groom's name*) to join in marriage. Love is a miraculous gift, and a wedding is a celebration of that magic, and that's why we are here today, to share in that magic!

Declaration of Intent

(*Groom's name*), Do you take (*Bride's name*) to be your wife, to love, honor, comfort and cherish, from this day forward?

(Groom answers: "I Do")

(*Bride's name*), Do you take (*Groom's name*) to be your husband, to love, honor, comfort and cherish, from this day forward?

(Bride answers: "I Do")

Ring Exchange

And now, seal your promises with these rings, the symbol of the life you share together.

(Groom's name), repeat after me;

(Bride's name), this ring is a symbol, of my promise, to always be, your lover, companion, and friend.

(Bride's name), repeat after me;

(Groom's name), this ring is a symbol, of my promise, to always be, your lover, companion, and friend.

Pronouncement of Marriage

Now, because you have chosen one another, and vowed to love each other in marriage, it gives me great joy to pronounce you husband and wife.

You may kiss.

I introduce to you, (*Groom's name*) and (*Bride's name*) (*last name*)

Traditional (Spiritual) Ceremony

Approval Blessing

(*To the Bride's Father, or other special people giving blessing, or all people in attendance*)

> Who gives their blessing on this union between (*Bride's name*) and (*Groom's name*)?

(*Response*) (I do/We do).

Welcome/Introduction

> (*Bride's name*) and (*Groom's name*), today you are surrounded by your family and friends. All of whom are gathered to witness your exchange of vows and to share in the joy of this occasion. Let this be a statement of what you mean to each other, and the commitment of marriage that you will make.

Address

> As you know, no one person can marry you. Only you can marry yourselves. By a mutual commitment to love each other, to work toward creating an atmosphere of care, consideration and respect, by a willingness to face life's anxieties together, you can make your wedded life your strength.

> On this day of your wedding you stand somewhat apart from other people. You stand within the light of your love; and this is as it should be. You will experience a lot together, some wonderful, some difficult. But even when it is difficult you must manage to call

upon the strength in the love you have for each other to see you through. From this day onward you must come closer together than ever before, you must love one another with the strength that makes this bond a marriage. As you exchange your vows, remember that the sensual part of love is great, but when this is combined with real friendship both are infinitely enhanced.

Dedication Blessing

I would like at this time to speak of some things which we pray for you. First, we pray for you a love that continues to give you joy and peace that provides you with energy to face the responsibilities of life. We pray for you a home of serenity, not just a place of private joy and retreat, but a temple wherein the values of God and family are generated and upheld. Finally, we pray that as you grow together, you are able to look back at your lives together, and say these two things to each other: Because you loved me, you have given me faith in myself; because I have seen the good in you, I have received from you a faith in humanity.

Declaration of Intent

(To the groom)

(*Groom's name*), Do you promise (*Bride's name*), that from this day onward you will stand with her in sickness and health, in joy and sorrow, and do you pledge to her your respect and your love?

(Groom) I do.

(To the bride)

(*Bride's name*), Do you promise (*Groom's name*), that from this day onward you will stand with him in sickness and health, in joy and sorrow, and do you pledge to him your respect and your love?

> *(Bride) I do.*

Reading

(A special selection of your choice. See the "Reading Selections" section of this book.)

Vows

(*Groom's name*), repeat after me.

> (Bride's name), today we begin our lives together.
> I promise before God, our families and our friends
> to be your faithful husband.
> I choose to live with you, as your lover, companion and friend,
> loving you when life is peaceful, and when it is painful,
> during our successes, and during our failures,
> supported by your strengths, and accepting your weaknesses.
> I will honor your goals and dreams,
> trying always, to encourage your fulfillment.
> I will strive to be honest, and open with you,
> sharing my thoughts, and my life with you.
> I promise to love and cherish you
> from this day forward.

(*Bride's name*), repeat after me.

> (Groom's name), today we begin our lives together.
> I promise before God, our families and our friends
> to be your faithful wife.
> I choose to live with you, as your lover, companion and friend,
> loving you when life is peaceful, and when it is painful,
> during our successes, and during our failures,
> supported by your strengths, and accepting your weaknesses.
> I will honor your goals and dreams,
> trying always, to encourage your fulfillment.
> I will strive to be honest, and open with you,
> sharing my thoughts, and my life with you.
> I promise to love and cherish you
> from this day forward.

Ring Blessing

These rings are an outward and visible sign of an inward and spiritual grace. Signifying to all the uniting of (*Bride's name*) and (*Groom's name*) in the bond of matrimony. In the presence of God and these friends, seal your promises with rings, the symbol of the life you share together.

Exchanging of the Rings

(*Groom's name*), repeat after me.

(*Bride's name*), In token and pledge, of the vow made between us, with this ring, I thee wed.

(*Bride's name*), repeat after me.

> (*Groom's name*), In token and pledge, of the vow made between us, with this ring, I thee wed.

Prayer

(A prayer selection of your choice, or have a friend or family member say one. See the spiritual "Reading Selections" section of this book.)

Candle Lighting Ceremony

(The bride and groom light a Unity candle with tapers that are already lit. See the "Candle Lighting Ceremony" section of this book.)

Pronouncement of Marriage

> (*Bride's name*) and (*Groom's name*) on behalf of all those present, and by the strength of your own love, I pronounce you married, and may the blessing of God be with you.

You may kiss.

I introduce to you (*Bride's name*) and (*Groom's name*) (last name), husband and wife.

Traditional (Non-spiritual) Ceremony

Approval Blessing

[*To the Bride's Father, or other special people giving approval, or all people in attendance*]

Who gives their approval on this union between (*Bride's name*) and (*Groom's name*)?

(*Response*) (I do/We do).

Welcome/Introduction

(*Bride's name*) and (*Groom's name*), today you are surrounded by your family and friends. All of whom are gathered to witness your exchange of vows and to share in the joy of this occasion. Let this be a statement of what you mean to each other, and the commitment of marriage that you will make.

Address

As you know, no one person can marry you. Only you can marry yourselves. By a mutual commitment to love each other, to work toward creating an atmosphere of care, consideration and respect, by a willingness to face life's anxieties together, you can make your wedded life your strength.

On this day of your wedding you stand somewhat apart from other people. You stand within the light of your love; and this is as it should be. You will experience a lot together, some wonderful, some difficult. But even when it is difficult you must manage to call upon the strength in the love you have for each other to see you through. From this day onward you must come closer together than ever before, you must love one another with the strength that makes this bond a marriage. As you exchange your vows, remember that the sensual part of love is great, but when this is combined with real friendship both are infinitely enhanced.

Opening Wishes

I would like at this time to speak of some things which we wish for you. First, we wish for you a love that continues to give you joy and peace that provides you with energy to face the responsibilities of life. We wish for you a home of serenity, not just a place of private joy and retreat, but a sanctuary wherein the values of family are generated and upheld. Finally, we wish that as you grow together, you are able to look back at your lives together, and say these two things to each other: Because you loved me, you have given me faith in myself; because I have seen the good in you, I have received from you a faith in humanity.

Declaration of Intent

(To the groom)

(_Groom's name_), Do you promise (_Bride's name_), that from this day onward you will stand with her in sickness and health, in joy and sorrow, and do you pledge to her your respect and your love?

Response: I do.

(To the bride)

(_Bride's name_), Do you promise (_Groom's name_), that from this day onward you will stand with him in sickness and health, in joy and sorrow, and do you pledge to him your respect and your love?

Response: I do.

Reading

(A special selection of your choice. See the "Reading Selections" section of this book.)

Vows

(*Groom's name*), repeat after me.

> (*Bride's name*), today we begin our lives together.
> I promise before our families and friends
> to be your faithful husband.
> I choose to live with you, as your lover, companion and friend.
> Loving you when life is peaceful, and when it is painful,
> during our successes, and during our failures,
> supported by your strengths, and accepting your weaknesses.
> I will honor your goals and dreams,
> trying always, to encourage your fulfillment.
> I will strive to be honest, and open with you,
> sharing my thoughts, and my life with you.
> I promise to love and cherish you
> from this day forward.

(*Bride's name*), repeat after me.

> (*Groom's name*), today we begin our lives together.
> I promise before our families and our friends
> to be your faithful wife.
> I choose to live with you, as your lover, companion and friend.
> Loving you when life is peaceful, and when it is painful,
> during our successes, and during our failures,
> supported by your strengths, and accepting your weaknesses.

I will honor your goals and dreams,

trying always, to encourage your fulfillment.

I will strive to be honest, and open with you,

sharing my thoughts, and my life with you.

I promise to love and cherish you

from this day forward.

Ring Wishes

These rings are an outward and visible sign of an inward and loving commitment. Signifying to all the uniting of (*Bride's name*) and (*Groom's name*) in the bond of matrimony. In the presence of these friends, seal your promises with rings, the symbol of the life you share together.

Exchanging of the Rings

(*Groom's name*), repeat after me.

> (*Bride's name*), In token and pledge, of the vow made between us, with this ring, I thee wed.

(*Bride's name*), repeat after me.

> (*Groom's name*), In token and pledge, of the vow made between us, with this ring, I thee wed.

Candle Lighting Ceremony

(The bride and groom light a Unity candle with tapers that are already lit. See the "Candle Lighting Ceremony" section of this book.)

Pronouncement of Marriage

(*Bride's name*) and (*Groom's name*) on behalf of all those present, and by the strength of your own love, I pronounce you married.

You may kiss.

I introduce to you (*Bride's name*) and (*Groom's name*) (last name), husband and wife.

Contemporary (Spiritual) Ceremony

Welcome/Introduction

(*Bride's name*) and (*Groom's name*) have invited you here today to share with them in this joyous celebration of their love and desire to join their lives together in marriage. We are here to rejoice and remember that it is love that leads us to our true destinations and to celebrate with (_Bride's name_) and (_Groom's name_) on their arrival in love and respect at this altar.

We are here to celebrate the marriage of (_Bride's name_) and (_Groom's name_), to honor the beginning of their new life.

We're here to listen, to love, to dance and celebrate, and to send them into their future with one outrageous, gigantic blessing. So sit back now, open your hearts, and let the wedding begin!

Opening Blessing

Marriage is a very special place, the sheltered environment in which we can endlessly explore ourselves in the presence of another and in which we can offer the possibility of true reflection of another. May the vision that (_Bride's name_) and (_Groom's name_) have of one another be always informed by the radiant force that first brought them together, and we pray that as they move into the sacredness of marriage that they always hold one another in the light of all light, and the love of all love.

Candles for Parents

Marriage is a venture of faith. It is a life of loving, comforting, honoring and keeping. (_Bride's name_) and (_Groom's name_) bring to this venture their unique history, personality and spirit. Part of their history was shared with their loved ones who have passed on. In memory of their lives and spirits, they light these candles in our midst, in celebration of this marriage.

[Groom lights candle]   (_Groom's name_), will now light a candle, in memory of (_Names of loved ones to be remembered_).

[Bride lights candle] (*Bride's name*), will now light a candle, in memory of (*Names of loved ones to be remembered*).

Reading

And now (*Friend's name*) will read a selection chosen by (*Bride's name*) and (*Groom's name*).

(A special selection of your choice. See the "Reading Selections" section of this book.)

Song

And now (*Friend's name*) will (sing/perform) a song chosen by (*Bride's name*) and (*Groom's name*).

(A special selection of your choice. See the "Music in the Ceremony" section of this book.)

Address

Marriage symbolizes the ultimate intimacy between a man and a woman, yet this closeness should not diminish but strengthen the individuality of each partner. A marriage that lasts is one that always has a little more to grow. It is out of the resonance between individuality and union that love, whose incredible strength is equal only to its incredible fragility, is born and reborn.

Marriage is a lifetime commitment, which recognizes the negative as well as the positive aspects of life. Marriage's content is never predetermined. It is a living organism that reflects the continuous choices of the individuals involved. In marrying we promise to love not only as we feel right now, but also as we intend to feel. In marriage we say not only, "I love you today," but also, "I promise to love you tomorrow, the next day and always."

Love doesn't limit. Love brings with it the gift of freedom. Love teaches us to encourage the people we love to make their own choices, seek their own path and learn their lessons in their own way and in their own time. Love also teaches us to share our feelings and thoughts with each other about those choices. We can then make decisions openly and freely, through our love that allows both to grow. Love that restrains is not love. To restrain another in the name of love, doesn't create love, it creates restraint.

Love means each person is free to follow his or her own heart. If we truly love, our choices will naturally and freely serve that love well. When we give freedom to another, we really give freedom to ourselves.

In promising always, we promise each other time. We promise to exercise our love, to stretch it large enough to embrace the unforeseen realities of the future. We promise to learn to love beyond the level of our instincts and inclinations, to love in hard times as well as when we are exhilarated by the pleasures of romance.

We change because of these promises. We shape ourselves according to them; we live in their midst and live differently because of them. We feel protected because of them. We try some things and resist trying others because, having promised, we feel secure—to see, to be, to love. Our souls are protected; our hearts have come home.

When we are safe in marriage, we can risk. Because we know we are loved, we can step beyond our fears; because we have chosen, we can transcend our insecurities. We can make mistakes, knowing we will not be cast out; take missteps, knowing someone will be there to catch us. And because mistakes and missteps are the stuff of change, of expansion, in marriage we can expand to our fullest capacity.

So remember these things, as you go out into the world as a couple: that your love will have seasons, that your relationship is a progression, and that love will prevail. Remembering each other, holding each other in your hearts and your minds, will give you a marriage as deep in its joy, as your courtship has been in its magic.

Congratulations (*Bride's name*) and (*Groom's name*), the real fun has just begun.

Dedication Blessing

Enfolded in joy, inhabited by hope, bathed in the infinite spectrum of light that is love, may you always be infused with it and beautifully illuminated by it. May every desire you have for your love be fulfilled. May your vision clearly behold one another. May you hear each other most genuinely. And may you give of your endless generosity of spirit to nourish one another's soul and sweetly keep the promises you make here today.

Declaration of Intent

(*Bride's name*) and (*Groom's name*), you have declared your intention to make this venture of faith and love, realizing that from this time forward your destinies will be woven of one design and your challenges and joys will be shared together. Today you are making public, before family and friends, that the words, "I love you," are a full commitment of yourselves, one to the other.

Understanding that marriage is the convergence of your individual and joint destinies as well as the greatest support for them,

(*Groom's name*), do you choose to marry, (*Bride's name*) and have her as your wife.
> *Response:* I do

(*Bride's name*), do you choose to marry, (*Groom's name*) and have him as your husband.
> *Response:* I do

Vows

(Bride's name), Repeat after me:
> I choose you, (*Groom's name*),

To be my husband, from this time forward.
To love you, and be faithful to you,
To be a comfort, in your life,
To nourish you, with my gentleness,
To uphold you, with my strength,
To love your body, as it ages,
To weigh the effects, of the words I speak
And of the things I do,
To never take you for granted,
But always give thanks, for your presence.
I promise you this, from my heart,
With my soul,
For all the days of my life.

(*Groom's name*), *Repeat after me:*

I choose you, (*Bride's name*),
To be my wife, from this time forward.
To love you, and be faithful to you,
To be a comfort, in your life,
To nourish you, with my gentleness,
To uphold you, with my strength,
To love your body, as it ages,
To weigh the effects, of the words I speak
And of the things I do,
To never take you for granted,
But always give thanks, for your presence.
I promise you this, from my heart,
With my soul,
For all the days of my life.

Ring Blessing

Rings are made precious by our wearing them. The rings you exchange at your wedding are the most special because they say that even in your uniqueness you have chosen to share your lives, to allow the presence of another human being to enhance who you are.

As you wear them through time, they will reflect not only who you are, but also what you have created together.

Exchange of Rings

(Groom's name), Repeat after me:

> I give you this ring, as a symbol of my love.
> And as a constant reminder,
> That I have chosen you, above all others,
> To be the one, to share my life.

(Bride's name), Repeat after me:

> I give you this ring, as a symbol of my love.
> And as a constant reminder,
> That I have chosen you, above all others,
> To be the one, to share my life.

Pronouncement of Marriage

(Bride's name) and *(Groom's name)*, because you have pledged your love and commitment to each other before these witnesses, I declare that you are husband and wife. May the spirit that lives in and around all of us fill your hearts and bless your lives.

The Kiss

You may now kiss to seal this union.

Closing Blessing

May you be blessed, every step of your path. May you endlessly delight one another. May you rest in the comfort of knowing that you have chosen through one another to serve the highest purposes of love. Depart in peace, recognizing that what you undertake together will bring you infinite joy.

Presentation

It is my pleasure to introduce to you, (_Bride's name_) and (_Groom's name_), (last name), husband and wife.

Contemporary (Non-spiritual) Ceremony

Welcome/Introduction

(_Bride's name_) and (_Groom's name_) have invited you here today to share with them in this joyous celebration of their love and desire to join their lives together in marriage. We are here to rejoice and remember that it is love that leads us to our true destinations and to celebrate with (_Bride's name_) and (_Groom's name_) on their arrival in love and respect at this altar.

We are here to celebrate the marriage of (_Bride's name_) and (_Groom's name_), to honor the beginning of their new life.

We're here to listen, to love, to dance and celebrate, and to send them into their future with our outrageous, loving, support. So sit back now, open your hearts, and let the wedding begin!

Opening Blessing

Marriage is a very special place, the sheltered environment in which we can endlessly explore ourselves in the presence of another and in which we can offer the possibility of true reflection of another. May the vision that (*Bride's name*) and (*Groom's name*) have of one another be always informed by the radiant force that first brought them together, and we wish that as they move into the sanctity of marriage that they always hold one another in the love of all love.

Candles for Parents

Marriage is a venture of faith. It is a life of loving, comforting, honoring and keeping. (*Bride's name*) and (*Groom's name*) bring to this venture their unique history and personality. Part of their history was shared with their loved ones who have passed on. In memory of their lives, they light these candles in our midst, in celebration of this marriage.

[Groom lights candle]   (*Groom's name*), will now light a candle, in memory of (*Names of loved ones to be remembered*).

[Bride lights candle]   (*Bride's name*), will now light a candle, in memory of (*Names of loved ones to be remembered*).

Reading

And now (*Friend's name*) will read a selection chosen by (*Bride's name*) and (*Groom's name*).

(A special selection of your choice. See the "Reading Selections" section of this book.)

Song

And now (*Friend's name*) will (sing/perform) a song chosen by (*Bride's name*) and (*Groom's name*).

(A special selection of your choice. See the "Music in the Ceremony" section of this book.)

Address

Marriage symbolizes the ultimate intimacy between a man and a woman, yet this closeness should not diminish but strengthen the individuality of each partner. A marriage that lasts is one that always has a little more to grow. It is out of the resonance between individuality and union that love, whose incredible strength is equal only to its incredible fragility, is born and reborn.

Marriage is a lifetime commitment, which recognizes the negative as well as the positive aspects of life. Marriage's content is never predetermined. It is a living organism that reflects the continuous choices of the individuals involved. In marrying we promise to love not only as we feel right now, but also as we intend to feel. In marriage we say not only, "I love you today," but also, "I promise to love you tomorrow, the next day and always."

Love doesn't limit. Love brings with it the gift of freedom. Love teaches us to encourage the people we love to make their own choices, seek their own path and learn their lessons in their own way and in their own time. Love also teaches us to share our feelings and thoughts with each other about those choices. We can then make decisions openly and freely, through our love that allows both to grow. Love that restrains is not love. To restrain another in the name of love, doesn't create love, it creates restraint. Love means each person is free to follow his or her own heart. If we truly love, our choices will naturally and freely serve that love well. When we give freedom to another, we really give freedom to ourselves.

In promising always, we promise each other time. We promise to exercise our love, to stretch it large enough to embrace the unforeseen realities of the future. We promise to learn to love beyond the level of our instincts and inclinations, to love in hard times as well as when we are exhilarated by the pleasures of romance.

We change because of these promises. We shape ourselves according to them; we live in their midst and live differently because of them. We feel protected because of them. We try some things and resist trying others because, having promised, we feel secure—to see, to be, to love. We are protected; our hearts have come home.

When we are safe in marriage, we can risk. Because we know we are loved, we can step beyond our fears; because we have chosen, we can transcend our insecurities. We can make mistakes, knowing we will not be cast out; take missteps, knowing someone will be there to catch us. And because mistakes and missteps are the stuff of change, of expansion, in marriage we can expand to our fullest capacity.

So remember these things, as you go out into the world as a couple: that your love will have seasons, that your relationship is a progression, and that love will prevail. Remembering each other, holding each other in your hearts and your minds, will give you a marriage as deep in its joy, as your courtship has been in its magic.

Congratulations (*Bride's name*) and (*Groom's name*), the real fun has just begun.

Opening Wishes

Enfolded in joy, inhabited by hope, bathed in the infinite spectrum of love, may you always be infused with it and beautifully enlightened by it. May every desire you have for your love be fulfilled. May your vision clearly behold one another. May you hear each other most genuinely. And may you give of your endless generosity to nourish one another's hearts and sweetly keep the promises you make here today.

Declaration of Intent

(*Bride's name*) and (*Groom's name*), you have declared your intention to make this venture of faith and love, realizing that from this time forward your destinies will be woven of one design and your challenges and joys will be shared together. Today you are making public, before family and friends, that the words, "I love you," are a full commitment of yourselves, one to the other.

Understanding that marriage is the convergence of your individual and joint destinies as well as the greatest support for them,

(*Groom's name*), do you choose to marry, (*Bride's name*) and have her as your wife.
> *Response:* I do

(*Bride's name*), do you choose to marry, (*Groom's name*) and have him as your husband.
> *Response:* I do

Vows

(*Bride's name*), *Repeat after me:*
> I choose you, (*Groom's name*),
> To be my husband, from this time forward.
> To love you, and be faithful to you,
> To be a comfort, in your life,
> To nourish you, with my gentleness,
> To uphold you, with my strength,
> To love your body, as it ages,
> To weigh the effects, of the words I speak
> And of the things I do,
> To never take you for granted,
> But always give thanks, for your presence.
> I promise you this, from my heart,
> For all the days of my life.

(*Groom's name*), *Repeat after me:*
> I choose you, (*Bride's name*),
> To be my wife, from this time forward.
> To love you, and be faithful to you,
> To be a comfort, in your life,
> To nourish you, with my gentleness,

To uphold you, with my strength,
To love your body, as it ages,
To weigh the effects, of the words I speak
And of the things I do,
To never take you for granted,
But always give thanks, for your presence.
I promise you this, from my heart,
For all the days of my life.

Ring Wishes

Rings are made precious by our wearing them. The rings you exchange at your wedding are the most special because they say that even in your uniqueness you have chosen to share your lives, to allow the presence of another human being to enhance who you are. As you wear them through time, they will reflect not only who you are, but also what you have created together.

Exchange of Rings

(Groom's name), Repeat after me:

I give you this ring, as a symbol of my love
And as a constant reminder
That I have chosen you, above all others
To be the one, to share my life.

(Bride's name), Repeat after me:

I give you this ring, as a symbol of my love
And as a constant reminder
That I have chosen you, above all others
To be the one, to share my life.

Pronouncement of Marriage

(*Bride's name*) and (*Groom's name*), because you have pledged your love and commitment to each other before these witnesses, I declare that you are husband and wife. May the love that lives in and around all of us fill your hearts and infuse your lives.

The Kiss

You may now kiss to seal this union.

Closing Wishes

May you be supported, every step of your path. May you endlessly delight one another. May you rest in the comfort of knowing that you have chosen through one another to serve the highest purposes of love. Depart in peace, recognizing that what you undertake together will bring you infinite joy.

Presentation

It is my pleasure to introduce to you, (*Bride's name*) and (*Groom's name*), (last name), husband and wife.

Traditional Renewal (Non-spiritual) Ceremony

Approval Blessing

[*To all people in attendance*]

Who gives their approval and support for this renewal between (*Bride's name*) and (*Groom's name*)?

(*Response*) We do.

Welcome/Introduction

(*Bride's name*) and (*Groom's name*), today you are surrounded by your family and friends, all of whom are gathered to witness your exchange of vows and to share in the joy of this occasion. Let this be a statement of what you mean to each other, and the renewal of vows that you will make.

Address

As you know, no one person can marry you. Only you can marry yourselves. By a mutual commitment to love each other, to work toward creating an atmosphere of care, consideration and respect, by a willingness to face life's anxieties together, you can make your wedded life your strength.

On this day of your wedding renewal you stand somewhat apart from other people. You stand within the light of your love; and this is as it should be. You will experience a lot together, some wonderful, some difficult. But even when it is difficult you must manage to call upon the strength in the love you have for each other to see you through. From this day onward you must come closer together than ever before, you must love one another with the strength that makes this bond a marriage. As you exchange your vows, remember that the sensual part of love is great, but when this is combined with real friendship both are infinitely enhanced.

Opening Wishes

I would like at this time to speak of some things which we wish for you. First, we wish for you a love that continues to give you joy and peace that provides you with energy to face the responsibilities of life. We wish for you a home of serenity, not just a place of private joy and retreat, but a sanctuary wherein the values of family are generated and upheld. Finally, we wish that as you grow together, you are able to look back at your lives together, and say these two things to each other: Because you loved me, you have given me faith in myself; because I have seen the good in you, I have received from you a faith in humanity.

Declaration of Intent

(To the groom)

(_Groom's name_), Do you promise (_Bride's name_), that from this day onward you will stand with her in sickness and health, in joy and sorrow, and do you pledge to her your respect and your love?

    (Response) I do.

(To the bride)

(_Bride's name_), Do you promise (_Groom's name_), that from this day onward you will stand with him in sickness and health, in joy and sorrow, and do you pledge to him your respect and your love?

    (Response) I do.

Reading

(A special selection of your choice. See the "Reading Selections" section of this book.)

Vows

(*Groom's name*), repeat after me.

> (*Bride's name*), today we renew our lives together.
> I promise before our families and friends
> to continue to be your faithful husband.
> I choose to live with you, as your lover, companion and friend,
> loving you when life is peaceful, and when it is painful,
> during our successes, and during our failures,
> supported by your strengths, and accepting your weaknesses.
> I will honor your goals and dreams,
> trying always, to encourage your fulfillment.
> I will strive to be honest, and open with you,
> sharing my thoughts, and my life with you.
> I promise to love and cherish you
> from this day forward.

(*Bride's name*), repeat after me.

> (*Groom's name*), today we renew our lives together.
> I promise before our families and our friends
> to continue to be your faithful wife.
> I choose to live with you, as your lover, companion and friend,
> loving you when life is peaceful, and when it is painful,
> during our successes, and during our failures,
> supported by your strengths, and accepting your weaknesses.

I will honor your goals and dreams,
trying always, to encourage your fulfillment.
I will strive to be honest, and open with you,
sharing my thoughts, and my life with you.
I promise to love and cherish you
from this day forward.

Ring Wishes

These rings are an outward and visible reminder of an inward and loving commitment, signifying to all the re-uniting of (_Bride's name_) and (_Groom's name_) in the bond of matrimony. In the presence of these friends, seal your promises with rings, the symbol of the life you share together.

Exchanging of the Rings

(_Groom's name_), repeat after me.

(_Bride's name_), In token and pledge, of the vow made between us, with this ring, I thee wed.

(_Bride's name_), repeat after me.

(_Groom's name_), In token and pledge, of the vow made between us, with this ring, I thee wed.

Candle Lighting Ceremony

(The bride and groom light a Unity candle with tapers that are already lit. See the "Candle Lighting Ceremony" section of this book.)

Pronouncement of Marriage

(*Bride's name*) and (*Groom's name*) on behalf of all those present, and by the strength of your own love, your commitment has been renewed.

You may kiss.

Contemporary Renewal (Non-spiritual) Ceremony

Welcome/Introduction

(*Bride's name*) and (*Groom's name*) have invited you here today to share with them in this joyous celebration of their love and desire to renew their vows in marriage. We are here to rejoice and remember that it is love that leads us to our true destinations and to celebrate with (*Bride's name*) and (*Groom's name*) on their arrival in love and respect at this altar.

We are here to celebrate the marriage of (*Bride's name*) and (*Groom's name*), to honor the renewal of their life together.

We're here to listen, to love, to dance and celebrate, and to send them into their new future with our outrageous, loving, support. So sit back now, open your hearts, and let the wedding begin!

Opening Blessing

Marriage is a very special place, the sheltered environment in which we can endlessly explore ourselves in the presence of another and in which we can offer the possibility of true reflection of another. May the vision that (*Bride's name*) and (*Groom's name*) have of one another be always informed by the radiant force that first brought them together, and we wish that as they continue in the sanctity of marriage that they always hold one another in the love of all love.

Candles for Parents

Marriage is a venture of faith. It is a life of loving, comforting, honoring and keeping. (*Bride's name*) and (*Groom's name*) bring to this venture their unique history and personality. Part of their history was shared with their loved ones who have passed on. In memory of their lives, they light these candles in our midst, in celebration of this marriage.

[Groom lights candle]   (*Groom's name*), will now light a candle, in memory of (*Names of loved ones to be remembered*).

[Bride lights candle]   (*Bride's name*), will now light a candle, in memory of (*Names of loved ones to be remembered*).

Reading

And now (*Friend's name*) will read a selection chosen by (*Bride's name*) and (*Groom's name*).

(A special selection of your choice. See the "Reading Selections" section of this book.)

Song

And now (*Friend's name*) will (sing/perform) a song chosen by (*Bride's name*) and (*Groom's name*).

(A special selection of your choice. See the "Music in the Ceremony" section of this book.)

Address

Marriage symbolizes the ultimate intimacy between a man and a woman, yet this closeness should not diminish but strengthen the individuality of each partner. A marriage that lasts is one that always has a little more to grow. It is out of the resonance between individuality and union that love, whose incredible strength is equal only to its incredible fragility, is born and reborn.

Marriage is a lifetime commitment which recognizes the negative as well as the positive aspects of life. Marriage's content is never predetermined. It is a living organism that reflects the continuous choices of the individuals involved. In marrying we promise to love not only as we feel right now, but also as we intend to feel. In marriage we say not only, "I love you today," but also, "I promise to love you tomorrow, the next day and always."

Love doesn't limit. Love brings with it the gift of freedom. Love teaches us to encourage the people we love to make their own choices, seek their own path and learn their lessons in their own way and in their own time. Love also teaches us to share our feelings and thoughts with each other about those choices. We can then make decisions openly and freely, through our love, that allows both to grow. Love that restrains is not love. To restrain another in the name of love, doesn't create love, it creates restraint.

Love means each person is free to follow his or her own heart. If we truly love, our choices will naturally and freely serve that love well. When we give freedom to another, we really give freedom to ourselves.

In promising always, we promise each other time. We promise to exercise our love, to stretch it large enough to embrace the unforeseen realities of the future. We promise to learn to love beyond the level of our instincts and inclinations, to love in hard times as well as when we are exhilarated by the pleasures of romance.

We change because of these promises. We shape ourselves according to them; we live in their midst and live differently because of them. We feel protected because of them. We try some things and resist trying others because, having promised, we feel secure—to see, to be, to love. We are protected; our hearts have come home.

When we are safe in marriage, we can risk. Because we know we are loved, we can step beyond our fears; because we have chosen, we can transcend our insecurities. We can make mistakes, knowing we will not be cast out; take missteps, knowing someone will be there to catch us. And because mistakes and missteps are the stuff of change, of expansion, in marriage we can expand to our fullest capacity.

So remember these things, as you go out into the world as a couple: that your love will have seasons, that your relationship is a progression, and that love will prevail. Remembering each other, holding each other in your hearts and your minds, will give you a marriage deep in its joy.

Congratulations (_Bride's name_) and (_Groom's name_), the real fun has just begun.

Opening Wishes

Enfolded in joy, inhabited by hope, bathed in the infinite spectrum of love, may you always be infused with it and beautifully enlightened by it. May every desire you have for your love be fulfilled. May your vision clearly behold one another. May you hear each other most genuinely. And may you give of your endless generosity to nourish one another's hearts and sweetly keep the promises you make here today.

Declaration of Intent

(*Bride's name*) and (*Groom's name*), you have declared your intention to renew this venture of faith and love, remembering that your destinies will continue to be woven of one design and your challenges and joys will be shared together. Today you are making public, before family and friends, that the words, "I love you," are a full commitment of yourselves, one to the other.

Understanding that marriage is the convergence of your individual and joint destinies as well as the greatest support for them,

(*Groom's name*), do you choose to renew your commitment to (*Bride's name*) as her husband?
>   *Response:* I do

(*Bride's name*), do you choose to renew your commitment to (*Groom's name*) as his wife?
>   *Response:* I do

Vows

(Bride's name), Repeat after me:
>   I choose you, (*Groom's name*),
>   To be my husband.
>   To love you, and be faithful to you,
>   To be a comfort, in your life.
>   To nourish you, with my gentleness,
>   To uphold you, with my strength,
>   To love your body, as it ages,
>   To weigh the effects, of the words I speak
>   And of the things I do,
>   To never take you for granted,

But always give thanks, for your presence.
I promise you this, from my heart,
For all the days of my life.

(Groom's name), Repeat after me:
I choose you, (*Bride's name*),
To be my wife.
To love you, and be faithful to you,
To be a comfort, in your life.
To nourish you, with my gentleness,
To uphold you, with my strength,
To love your body, as it ages,
To weigh the effects, of the words I speak
And of the things I do,
To never take you for granted,
But always give thanks, for your presence.
I promise you this, from my heart,
For all the days of my life.

The Kiss

You may now kiss to seal the renewal of this union.

Closing Wishes

May you be supported, every step of your path. May you endlessly delight one another. May you rest in the comfort of knowing that you have chosen through one another to serve the highest purposes of love. Depart in peace, recognizing that what you undertake together will bring you infinite joy.

ZEN Ceremony

Welcome/Introduction

We have come together for the marriage of (*Groom's name*) and (*Bride's name*).

Address

Marriage begins in the giving of words. We cannot join ourselves to one another without giving our word. And this must be an unconditional giving, for in joining ourselves to one another we join ourselves to the unknown.

(*Groom's name*) and (*Bride's name*), you are about to take a new step forward into life. This day is made possible not only because of your love for each other, but through the grace of your parents and all of humanity.

Courtesy and consideration, even in anger and adversity, are the seeds of compassion. Love is the fruit of compassion. Trust, love, and respect are the sustaining virtues of marriage. They enable us to learn from each situation, and help us to realize that everywhere we turn we meet our Self.

We nourish ourselves and each other in living by the following five precepts:

1. We allow the fullest expression of our deepest Self.
2. We take full responsibility for our own life, in all its infinite dimensions.
3. We affirm our trust in the honesty and wisdom of our soul, which with our love and reverence always shows us the true way.
4. We are committed to embrace all parts of our Self, including our deepest fears and shadows, so that they may be transformed into light.

5. We affirm our willingness to keep our hearts open, even in the midst of great pain.

Dedication Blessing

May your fulfillment and joy in each other and in yourselves increase with every passing year. And, may you continue to deepen your life with each other and with all conscious beings.

Reading 1

And now (*Friend's name*) will read a selection chosen by (*Bride's name*) and (*Groom's name*).

> (*A special selection of your choice. See the "Reading Selections" section of this book.*)

Vows

Now (*Bride's name*) and (*Groom's name*) will exchange their marriage vows.

(*Groom's name*), *Repeat after me*

> I, (*Groom's name*), take you, (*Bride's name*) to be my wife, in equal love, as a mirror for my true Self, as a partner on my path, to honor and to cherish, in sorrow and in joy, till death do us part.

(*Bride's name*), *Repeat after me*

> I, (*Bride's name*), take you, (*Groom's name*) to be my husband, in equal love, as a mirror for my true Self, as a partner on my path, to honor and to cherish, in sorrow and in joy, till death do us part.

Reading 2

And now (*Friend's name*) will read a selection chosen by (*Bride's name*) and (*Groom's name*).

> (*A special selection of your choice. See the "Reading Selections" section of this book.*)

Ring Exchange

Now (*Bride's name*) and (*Groom's name*) celebrate their love and proclaim their union with rings of precious metal. The precious nature of their rings represents the subtle and wonderful essence they find individually, through their mutual love, respect, and support. The metal itself represents the long life they may cultivate together, not only in years, but in all the infinite dimensions of each moment they share.

You may now exchange rings.

> [*Couple exchanges rings*]

Because of your choice to share a life and the vows made here today, I pronounce you, husband and wife.

You may kiss to seal this vow.

Celtic Ceremony

Celtic Wedding History

There were many rituals associated with wedding ceremonies among Celtic peoples. The most important aspect of all Celtic weddings was the feast. This included the families of the bride and groom as well as friends and members of the community. Unlike weddings today, which separate the wedding ceremony and the reception, Celts viewed the whole affair as one grand ceremony. The community was there to solidify the bond between the Bride and Groom. The Celtic bride was held in great esteem. The term "Bride" is Celtic in origin, coming from Brigid, the goddess and saint of Celtic lore.

Celtic weddings were simple and meaningful. They often took place outside in nature to bless the union. Nature was very important to the Celts. They believed the soul existed within and outside of an individual. The soul would manifest in the trees, the rocks, the waters and the sun. Humans and the world around them were intertwined, the soul connected to the spirit of the earth. Their belief in marriage was that two souls would join together so their strengths would be twice as great and hardships only half as difficult.

The ceremony itself was a very simple ritual called handfasting. The bride and groom would stand facing each other holding hands and they were bound by a ceremonial rope, cord, or wrap. This is where the term "tying the knot" comes from. This symbolically signified the unity of the couple. To finalize the marriage the couple would hold hands and jump over a branch or a broom into their new life together.

Celtic Ceremony #1

[If the ceremony takes place outdoors, trees, water and other natural elements provide an inspiring setting. If the ceremony takes place indoors, green branches from an oak tree, branches from an evergreen during winter months, and flowers will provide the proper spirit. An altar should be prepared which contains incense, three candles, a two foot length of silk rope, a chalice or cup and a pitcher filled with wine or ale and an oak branch (two feet in length is sufficient). The incense should be lit before the start of the ceremony.]

Welcome/Introduction

Friends, family and members of the community, welcome to this ceremony which will unite two souls in marriage.

Address

Marriage is an agreement, which should not be entered into lightly. It is the union of two souls, two hearts and two minds. The Celtic concept of the soul encompasses far more than we traditionally think of today. The Celtic belief of the soul exists within and outside the individual; it is manifest in the trees, the rocks, the waters and the Sun. The relationship between humanity and the world around them is intertwined. The soul is inextricably tied to the Universal spirit of the Earth.

Celtic Trinity Ceremony

The Celtic trinity is an ancient profession of faith that maintains that trust in the soul, belief in the heart and faith in the mind, are all that is needed to lead an honorable, loving and fulfilled life.

(*Bride's name*) and (*Groom's name*), in marriage, your souls will join together so that your strengths shall be twice as great and your hardships will be only half as difficult.

As you share the (ale/wine) from this wedding cup let it remind you to trust in your soul which is the Universal spirit. Trust in its strength and it will strengthen the bond between you.

[Officiant pours the wine or ale into the cup and hands it to the bride, who takes a sip and hands it to the groom who takes a sip, and hands it back to the Officiant.]

[Officiant then holds up the silk rope]

Please place your hands over one another.

Your open hands placed over one another represent your hearts. The silk rope represents the belief, which binds them together.

Belief in your heart is a testament to the power of love and compassion. Belief in your heart is the constant desire to put your spouse before you in every way, to act mindful and to allow love and patience to prevail. Belief in your heart will always guide your marriage and allow the power of love to grow, multiply and strengthen. At times, your souls may drift apart, but the belief in your heart will act as a silk tether, which will keep you together.

[Officiant then binds together their hands by wrapping the silk rope around them]

Having faith in your mind is the last concept of the Celtic trinity. May each of you maintain your independence of mind, respecting each other's thoughts and trying to learn from one another. May positive thoughts always guide you.

[Officiant lights the candles]

These candles represent the light that burns away the darkness of ignorance. May you always strive to keep your mind bright, sharp and uncluttered. Your mindfulness will add joy and ease to your marriage.

Vows

(*Groom's name*), *Repeat after me*

> I, (*Groom's name*), take (*Bride's name*), as my wife and vow to be mindful in our journey together, to love her and to cherish her, to trust in the Universal soul, to have belief in my heart and faith in my mind. From this day forward our souls will be as one.

(*Bride's name*), *Repeat after me*

> I, (*Bride's name*), take (*Groom's name*), as my husband and vow to be mindful in our journey together, to love him and cherish him, to trust in the Universal soul, to have belief in my heart and faith in my mind. From this day forward our souls will be as one.

Jumping the Branch

> *[Officiant holds up the branch]*

It is tradition to jump over a branch together to finalize the marriage. This symbolizes the transition into a new existence where you are committed to each other and to a life of growth and love.

> *[Officiant places the branch on the ground]*

(*Bride's name*) and (*Groom's name*), please join hands now and jump over the branch into your new life together.

> *[The couple jumps over the branch]*

Pronouncement

By the power vested in me by the State of (*State's Name*), I now declare you to be husband and wife.

The Kiss

You may kiss to seal this union.

Making It Legal

Who Can Perform Your Ceremony?

Most states in the US recognize licensed or ordained ministers, officiants, clergymen, priests, rabbis, pastors, judges and justices of the peace as authorized to perform marriage ceremonies. In some states government officials may be authorized to legally perform the ceremony. Contrary to some popular beliefs, no State currently authorizes ship captains to perform marriages.

Each State has its own criteria for who can legally perform a marriage ceremony. The following reference is a website that lists the criteria by State, but it is still recommended that you confirm with the County Clerk in the state where the wedding will take place to verify the current requirements.

Criteria by State:
http://marriage.about.com/cs/marriagelicenses/a/officiants.htm

If you know someone whom you would like to perform the ceremony, and they are not currently ordained, there are organizations that ordain ministers either online or through the mail (see the "How to Become Ordained" section of this book).

How to Become Ordained

Becoming an Officiant

An Officiant is someone who performs a religious rite or presides over a religious service or ceremony. It is simply another word for Clergy or Minister and commonly used to refer to people authorized to perform marriage ceremonies, especially for non-denominational and non-religious ceremonies.

The United States in general does not attempt to define what an organization must be in order to qualify as a Church or what qualifications are necessary to be a minister. This goes back to early American history and the separation of Church and State. Each religious denomination has its own requirements for becoming ordained.

If you wish to become ordained and are not affiliated with a particular religious denomination, there are several religious organizations in the U.S. that provide non-denominational ordination (no training necessary, sometimes a fee is charged). One of these organizations is Universal Life Church. By visiting their website and completing a form online, a person can become ordained for free with the click of a button and yes (as of this writing) it is legal in all 50 states (with the exception of New York *City*).

Website for Universal Life Church: http://www.ulc.net/

Some States require you to either register a Letter of Good Standing or a Copy of your credentials at the County Court house. Other States require you to request and file an application. It is recommended that you verify the requirements for the state where the ceremony will take place with the County Clerk prior to performing a marriage ceremony.

For information on Officiant requirements by state: http://usmarriagelaws.com/

Considerations When Selecting an Officiant

It is important to choose the Officiant (also known as "Minister") who best demonstrates the ability to carry out your desires. The words spoken at your ceremony should reflect what the two of you believe and feel. Here are some tips on what to consider when selecting an Officiant.

What is the Officiant's experience?

The government does not issue licenses to ministers, so an Officiant's experience with weddings is important. How many has he or she performed? Does the Officiant have references you can contact? Does the Officiant have credentials he or she can show you?

What is the spiritual or religious perspective of the Officiant?

Many ministers subscribe to the doctrines of a particular faith. If you are not of the same faith, let him or her know what your religious values are in the first meeting. Can they work with you to create a ceremony that is true to *your* beliefs, or do you feel that the

Officiant has an agenda to conform your ceremony into his or her particular denominational preferences? Will he or she work well with your beliefs?

How accommodating is the Officiant?

If you want a non-traditional song played during the ceremony, will the Officiant allow it? Are you free to add your own vows or other special, romantic touches? Do you want a little humor in the ceremony? Even if you don't know what kind of wedding ceremony you want, are you confident that the Officiant will allow for changes as the wedding day approaches? Will the Officiant allow flash photography during the wedding? Will the Officiant work with you to develop a ceremony, which honors your religious or non-religious traditions and beliefs?

What moral criteria does the Officiant expect you to meet?

If you and your fiancé are living together, already have children, are expecting a child, or if either of you have been through a divorce, it is important to tell the prospective Officiant your situation during your first phone conversation. Some Officiants will reject you immediately, or express other expectations and it is better to find this out early.

What about premarital counseling?

Some couples want counseling, and others do not feel it is necessary. Some Officiants offer excellent counseling programs, but others may pressure you into "counseling" programs that ask you to sign a tithing agreement or make a commitment to join a particular church and attend faithfully every week. Counseling programs offered by an Officiant as well as those offered independently, are only as good as your willingness to deeply participate. Some people definitely benefit from them, but many do not, especially if you are simply fulfilling an obligation by attending the sessions. The decision is yours, and the Officiant you select should respect and honor that decision.

How many meetings will you have?

Some Officiants say no meeting is necessary, that he or she will just show up for the wedding and you can run your own rehearsal. Others want you to go through their extensive premarital counseling. Some will offer one or two preparatory meetings and a rehearsal. Some are unwilling to meet with you in person if you are just "shopping around." What do you want? Can the Officiant meet your wishes? Will the Officiant be available to talk by phone as questions arise? What is your preferred method of working with them to create your ceremony? Are they willing to meet in person, or do they only work with you over the phone or via email?

Will the Officiant run the rehearsal?

An experienced Officiant at your wedding rehearsal can be very helpful, but he or she may not be available at the scheduled time. If the Officiant is unable or unwilling to attend the rehearsal, will other arrangements be made for someone to lead your wedding party through the steps? For more elaborate weddings, it is important to have someone available to guide you and your attendants through the practice of your ceremony, so that you know what to expect. Also, ask the Officiant if it is okay for the two of you to face one another during the ceremony (your guests will be able to see your faces instead of your backs).

What will the Officiant wear?

Some Officiants wear suits (a black suit is desirable as it blends in with any color scheme), some wear robes, and others wear a wide variety of garments from jeans and tennis shoes to butterfly wings (yes, someone actually showed up to perform a ceremony wearing butterfly wings)! Ask to see a picture of the clothing that will be worn on your wedding day, to determine if it looks suitable. If it is too ornate, or if it has prominent religious symbols, which may offend some family members, ask the Officiant if he or she would consider wearing a basic suit instead.

What ceremony choices does the Officiant offer?

Many officiants have only one ceremony they offer. Be sure you get to review their ceremony and ensure that it expresses what you want communicated at your wedding. Ask if they have any spontaneous words they will add. Some Officiants will have a few simple choices (with the option of adding some of your own ideas) so that you can create the ceremony that is the most meaningful to you. Others will design an elaborate, customized wedding just for you.

Ask how long they think the ceremony itself will take; this is important information for your facility, photographer, caterer, etc. You may prefer something simpler than what the Officiant is offering, or more flexible. Whatever you want, let the Officiant know in advance.

Is the Officiant focused on serving you?

Many people feel that they have to meet a minister's (also known as "Officiant") standards, and in some religious traditions this is entirely valid. But remember, the original meaning of the word "minister" is "servant." Is the minister serving your needs on your big day? Are you comfortable in their presence, or do you feel like you have to withhold things to prevent his or her disapproval? Do you feel pressured to behave differently to gain their approval? Find an Officiant who is eager to serve you, and your wedding day will be a beautiful one for everyone.

Obtaining the Marriage License

What is the difference between the Marriage License and the Marriage Certificate? The marriage *license* is a legal document, obtained by the couple, that authorizes a designated party to perform the ceremony, allowing you to get married; and the marriage *certificate* is the form filed with the State which officially certifies that the nuptials took place and once recorded is the official document that proves you are married (a certified copy may be requested from the State once the marriage has been recorded).

To determine the location and requirements to obtain a marriage license, contact the local marriage license county or city clerk office in the state where the marriage will take place.

For information on how to obtain your marriage license by state and county: http://www.marriagelicense.com/license.html

Marriage License Laws in the US

Each State has specific Marriage License laws for a couple to wed. Although there are differences between the requirements in the various states, a marriage performed in one state must be recognized by every other state under the Full Faith and Credit Clause of the United States Constitution.

The following reference is a website that lists the criteria by State, but it is still recommended that you confirm with the state where the wedding will take place to verify the current requirements.

For information on Marriage License Laws by State:
http://usmarriagelaws.com/

Filing the Paperwork

The couple receives the appropriate documents when they apply for their Marriage License. The couple then provides the Officiant with the Marriage License and Marriage Certificate documents prior to the wedding ceremony. A portion of the Marriage Certificate form will be completed by the couple in advance of the ceremony and the rest of it will be completed after the ceremony (i.e. signing the document and Officiant information).

After the marriage ceremony is performed, the Officiant (or person who performs the marriage ceremony) has a duty to send a copy of the Marriage Certificate to the county or state agency that records marriage certificates. The couple may then request a certified copy of the certificate from the county or state agency once the marriage has been recorded. Some Officiants will order a certified copy for the couple as an added service at the time they send in the paperwork.

Failure to send the marriage certificate to the appropriate agency does not necessarily nullify the marriage, but it may make proof of the marriage more difficult.

Worksheet for Creating Your Ceremony

Procession: Music Selection(s)

Song:_____

Song:_____

Song:_____

Song:_____

Song:_____

Song:_____

Reading(s)   Page #'s_____

Approval Blessing   Page #_____

Music Selection(s)

Song:_____

Song:_____

Reading(s)   Page #'s _____

Welcome/Introduction   Page #_____

Music Selection(s)

Song:_____

Song:_____

Reading(s)   Page #'s _____

Opening Blessing   Page #_____

Music Selection(s)

Song:_____

Song:_____

Reading(s)   Page #'s _____

The Address   Page #_____

Music Selection(s)

Song:_____

Song:_____

Reading(s)   Page #'s _____

Dedication Blessing   Page #_____

Music Selection(s)

Song:_____

Song:_____

Reading(s)   Page #'s _____

Declaration of Intent   Page #_____

Music Selection(s)

Song:_____

Song:_____

Reading(s)   Page #'s _____

The Vows   Page #_____

Music Selection(s)

Song:_____

Song:_____

Reading(s)   Page #'s _____

Ring Blessing   Page #_____

Music Selection(s)

Song:_____

Song:_____

Reading(s)   Page #'s _____

Exchanging of the Rings	Page #_____

Music Selection(s)

Song:_____

Song:_____

Reading(s)   Page #'s _____

Pronouncement of Marriage	Page #_____

Music Selection(s)

Song:_____

Song:_____

Reading(s)   Page #'s _____

The Kiss   Page #_____

Music Selection(s)

Song:_____

Song:_____

Reading(s)   Page #'s _____

Closing Blessing   Page #_____

Music Selection(s)

Song:_____

Song:_____

Reading(s)   Page #'s _____

The Presentation   Page #_____

Music Selection(s)

Song:_____

Song:_____

Reading(s)   Page #'s _____

The Recession: Music Selection(s)

Song:_____

Song:_____

Song:_____

Song:_____

Song:_____

Song:_____

Additional Ceremonies:

(Candle Lighting Ceremony, Rose Ceremony, Sand Ceremony, etc.)

Description:_____

Placement in Wedding:_____

Page #_____

Description: _____

Placement in Wedding:_____

Page #_____

Description: _____

Placement in Wedding:_____

Page #_____

Description: _____

Placement in Wedding:_____

Page #_____

Description: _____

Placement in Wedding:_____

Page #_____

Notes

Bibliography

Kingma, Daphne Rose. Weddings from the Heart: Ceremonies for an Unforgettable Wedding. Berkeley, CA: Conari, 1991. Print.

Oriah. The Invitation. San Francisco, CA: HarperOne, 1999. Print. All rights reserved. Presented with permission of the author www.oriah.org.

Williamson, Marianne. Illuminata: Thoughts, Prayers, Rites of Passage. New York: Random House, 1994. Print.

Biography

Dayna Reid, Writer, Executive, Minister. She has officiated weddings for over 12 years in addition to her full time job in the Information Technology industry. Her love for people and the desire to provide couples with a non-judgmental and personalized approach to selecting the words spoken at their wedding inspired her to seek ministry ordination. Although Dayna personally believes in God, she also believes, "Everyone has to find their own way in this world, including any beliefs they may have about the mysteries. Because truly, all we really have is a faith in what we believe to be true."

Made in the USA
Charleston, SC
23 September 2011